ARE YOU TALKING TO ME?

Are You Talking to Me?

Every Women's Guide to Hearing From God

KIM WIER

SERVANT PUBLICATIONS
ANN ARBOR, MICHIGAN

Vine Books is an imprint of Servant Publications especially designed to serve evangelical Christians.

Servant Publications—Mission Statement
We are dedicated to publishing books that spread the gospel of Jesus Christ, help Christians to live in accordance with that gospel, promote renewal in the church, and bear witness to Christian unity.

Servant Publications
P.O. Box 8617
Ann Arbor, MI 48107
www.servantpub.com

Cover design: Alan Furst Inc., Minneapolis, Minn.

02 03 04 05 10 9 8 7 6 5 4 3 2 1

Printed in the United States of America
ISBN 1-56955-331-9

Library of Congress Cataloging-in-Publication Data

Wier, Kim.
    Are you talking to me? : every woman's guide to hearing from God / Kim Wier.
        p. cm.
    ISBN 1-56955-331-9 (alk. paper)
    1. Christian women--Prayer-books and devotions--English. 2. Spiritual
    journals--Authorship. I. Title.
    BV4844 .W57 2002
    242'.643--dc21

                                                                    2002000306

~~~~~~~

How I Thank My God...

... for my husband who has indulged and encouraged my passion for answering God's call and given me a life I treasure.

... for my children who think I'm funny and give me so much to laugh about.

... for my mom, my friend and role model, who never stops teaching me, and for Cliff whose greatest lesson was unconditional love.

... for my dad, who was proud of me when my greatest accomplishment was a C+ in Geometry.

... for my big sister, who still puts up with me, and for her precious family.

... for those third-grade prayer warriors and all my friends at Fredonia Hill Baptist Academy.

... for a community of believers in this small Texas town who taught me the joy of hearing from God everyday.

Had God left out even one of you, I would be the lesser.

> *I thank my God every time I remember you. In all my prayers for all of you, I always pray with joy because of your partnership in the gospel from the first day until now ... It is right for me to feel this way about all of you since I have you in my heart.*
>
> PHILIPPIANS 1:3-6

Contents

Introduction

When I get into my car and strap on the seatbelt, I am living in a world all my own. Well, maybe not all my own. There are usually three kids, sometimes a dog, and occasionally a husband strapped in with me. The part about living there is accurate, though, if living includes eating, drinking, and spending almost every waking moment on four wheels. I seriously question why we invested so much in our house. It would have been more practical to buy a motor home and call it a day. As it stands, our home is still my husband's castle, and the car is my upholstered dungeon.

In it, I'm a slave to the school bell, baseball practice, the dry cleaners, and 1,001 other pressing appointments. It's like a little isolation booth, only I never get to be alone. Instead, I'm locked in with squabbling siblings, stale French fries, static on the radio, and sundry critters known to escape from my middle son's pockets.

No wonder the last police officer who pulled me over had to follow me six blocks before I noticed he was trying to get my attention. When I rolled down the window, the noise of a baby crying and two boys fighting over the last stick of gum almost knocked the poor guy off his feet. I must have seemed pathetic, because he let me off with a warning and a sympathetic look. He couldn't even give me those, though, until he had helped me search the car for my screaming baby's pacifier. Then I got the obligatory lecture about slowing down.

The man obviously was not married. Otherwise his wife would have set him straight. Every woman in America knows there is no way we can slow down. Each day is a race against time, hurdling pothole after pothole of obligations, duties, and chores before collapsing at the feet of our husbands' recliners. The only way to keep up is to keep moving.

Unfortunately, at that pace it's not only hard to hear a siren chasing you down the street, it's also hard to hear God over all that road noise. Yet, not since Jesus met Saul on the road to Damascus have we been more interested in hearing personally from God. The only question is, can we really hear the whisper of God over the whirlwind of life?

If Saul had found himself on the same roads we travel today, he would have encountered the same problems in hearing God that most American women face—too much noise, too little time, and gum stuck on the car seat. With the radio blasting and the kids fighting, Saul's response to God might have been, "Are you talking to me?"

Saul, though, had the luxury of being pulled over on a quiet rural road, where he would be sure to see the flash of light sent to get his attention. God was speaking to him loud and clear. Yet what are busy women in the twenty-first century to do if we want to hear what God has to say?

Since it is unlikely that, like Saul, we will be struck blind and sent into seclusion for three days (though that sounds pretty good) we have to train ourselves to hear God right in the middle of life's traffic jams. It can happen. When we deliberately focus on Him, every broken dish, scraped knee, missed deadline, and overdraw on the checking account can become an opportunity to meet God on the road and hear what He has to say.

Are You Talking to Me? is a collection of real-life adventures and collisions from my own road trips, as I learned to look in my rearview mirror to see if God was trying to get my attention. Many of them may seem like familiar scenes from your own life, but since they are always more amusing when they happen to someone else… I invite you to spend the next thirty-one days laughing along with me as together we learn to look for the spiritual side of everyday life. Each day's lighthearted devotion is punctuated with scriptures that reveal the spiritual truths God ticketed me with when He pulled me over. Each one is followed by a prayer of application that puts the day's lessons into practice in a real way.

Don't stop there, though. Now it's your turn. At the end of every day's devotion you will find journal pages to help you reflect on your own day and hear from God personally. What was funny? What made you cry? What is God saying to you through it all? Don't go to bed until you have thought through the events of your day and looked for God's flashing lights with prayers for reflection. You may be surprised what you hear.

You may discover that God wants to teach you about His faithfulness. Perhaps you will find that He wants to give you a warning. God might use the events of your day to give you encouragement, correction, or instruction. You won't know what He is saying, though, until you stop and listen. When you do, you will find that He is indeed talking to you. By the end of these thirty-one days, you will have developed the habit of expecting to hear from God in the midst of your everyday life and listening for what He has to say.

God wants to speak personally to you. He knows that your life is demanding and that you rush through it like a whirlwind. But if, like Elijah, you listen carefully, you, too, will hear Him speak.

[Elijah went to the mountain to hear from God.] "Then a great and powerful wind tore the mountains apart,... but the Lord was not in the wind.... There was an earthquake, but the Lord was not in the earthquake. After the earthquake came a fire, but the Lord was not in the fire. And after the fire came a gentle whisper. When Elijah heard it, he pulled his cloak over his face and went out.... Then a voice [spoke] to him."

1 KINGS 19:11-13

Elijah sought God, even over all the noise and fury around him. When he did, he was rewarded with a personal encounter, the gentle whisper of the living and loving God. If we are willing to do the same, to seek God and listen carefully, we, too, will be rewarded.

For the Lord searches every heart and understands every motive behind the thoughts. If you seek Him, He will be found by you.

1 CHRONICLES 28:9

If you want to hear what God has to say to you personally, seek Him on the everyday roads of your life. Whether you are hitting all the green lights or having a fender bender, you will find that God is indeed talking to you.

Together we will go on a thirty-one-day journey you will never forget. What are we waiting for? Let's hit the road.

Day 1
Taking the Bait

My neighbors are pests. I mean that literally. Some of them have six legs; some have eight. A few hop and some fly, but every single one is unwelcome.

I'm not sure when these undesirables moved into the area. One day I lived in a peaceful rural neighborhood, and the next day I was surrounded by bug gangs. The first to invade were the spiders.

We didn't mind so much when they just shared our porch. In the evening we would sit in the rockers and watch them weave their webs over the railing. Unlike the house pets, at least they were feeding themselves. Then one day I opened the front door and realized our eight-legged neighbors had set their sights on us. The web stretched across our doorway. That was only the beginning. Soon I found that spiders were under the living room chairs, behind furniture, and in corners. They were claiming squatter's rights with their little spider homesteads, rebuilding as fast as I could sweep them away.

While we were fighting off the enemy inside, a new pestilence began outside—frogs. They were everywhere. At first it was fun. Every night the kids went frog hunting. They caught two or three, then four or five, then eight, then ten—then we were kicking them out of the way just to get to the door.

Eventually, they attempted to drive us off the property with an FBI tactic (that's Frog Bureau of Intimidation). They blasted us night after night with croaking. It was psychological warfare. We could hear them, but we couldn't see them. It might have worked had we not been distracted by two other neighbors-turned-terrorists that infiltrated the perimeter.

First came giant flying roaches. I'm not talking about the kind that hides in the kitchen, eating everything your teenage boy hasn't. This variety dive-bombs you when you enter a room, eats entire bags of dog food, and, when you step on one, crunches loud enough to register on a Richter scale. We had hand-to-hand combat with these pests only a few times, but of all our confrontations, those were the most terrifying.

The most annoying pests were the ants that came marching in, and not one by one either. They took over my closet, my bathroom, and finally my bedroom. They outnumbered us one thousand to one. When I came home and saw them trying to carry off my cat, I knew we needed professional help.

Two days later the exterminator arrived with a license to kill. She appraised the situation and made a plan of attack. The frogs, she said, would leave at the end of the season, but the roaches and spiders had only minutes to make their peace as she sprayed poison in every nook and cranny. The ants would require a more subtle approach.

"There are too many ants to poison individually. So you have to let them destroy themselves," she said, as she whipped out attractive little ant hotels.

"Each one of these has bait that the ants can't resist. We'll just set them in front of the ants, and they will carry the bait back to their friends. Pretty soon they'll all be back for more."

She was right. Before long an ant assembly line had cleaned out all the bait trays. Within twenty-four hours my pesky neighbors were gone—most of them doomed by their own weakness, as they gave in to a temptation too great to resist. If only those ants had read their Bibles, they might be alive today.

No temptation has seized you except what is common to man. And God is faithful; he will not let you be tempted beyond what you can bear. But when you are tempted, he will also provide a way out so that you can stand up under it.

1 CORINTHIANS 10:13

OK, so maybe that wouldn't have helped the ants. Yet knowing Scripture certainly can help us. Through it we know that God is not the one who tempts us (see Jas 1:12-15). He does know our weaknesses, however, and at times allows those to be tested. Unfortunately, the Great Deceiver, who has been tempting mankind since the Garden, often sends those temptations in seemingly irresistible packages. What a comfort to know that God has given us a way to resist the bait.

Jesus modeled it for us as He turned from offers of fame and glory to the Word of God for strength and assurance (see Mt 4). He proved that temptation itself isn't sin. It is an opportunity to follow God as He leads the way out. And while God promises that we can overcome any temptation, like a pest, it is sure to return again and again. When it does, we can turn to the Professional for help.

Dear Lord,
You know my innermost being. There is no weakness I can hide from You. You know the things that tempt me to turn from the path of righteousness. Lord, strengthen me with Your Word and show me the way of escape when temptation threatens to overtake me.

How did God strengthen you today?
Turn the page and find out.

Are You Talking to Me?
~~~~~~~~

Logging the Miles   Today is _____

One word to describe my day would be _____

The greatest thing about today was _____

_____

_____

_____

_____

_____

The funniest thing that happened today was _____

_____

_____

_____

_____

_____

I was really frustrated by _____

_____

_____

_____

_____

_____

I wish I would have _____

_____

_____

_____

_____

Are You Talking to Me?
~~~~~~~~

God, I could tell that You were with me today because _____

_____

_____

_____

_____

_____

_____

I'm ready to hear You speak, Lord. What I hear You say through it all is

_____

_____

_____

_____

_____

_____

God, because I heard You, I know that I should _____

_____

_____

_____

_____

_____

_____

A scripture that comes to mind is _____

_____

_____

_____

_____

_____

Day 2
Dearly Departed

I t's settled. If I die tomorrow, an inheritance is secured for my family. They needn't worry about their future. I have a Will.

I won't pretend that I understand every nuance of the document, in part because everyone involved apparently gets a new name. My husband and I were the first to be rechristened. I am Testatrix. He is Executor. It sounds as if we are rulers from the planet Zorg.

All three of my children are henceforth to be known by one common name, Beneficiary. This one I may actually adopt at home. I might appear less senile if I could keep their names straight for a change. I sense their confidence in my mental capacity diminishing each time I tell Bailey to get his homework done, only to hear, "I'm Chase, Mom, remember?"

Now I can just say, "Don't argue with me, Beneficiary, I am Testatrix, ruler of intergalactic discipline."

It isn't just people who have been renamed. My mortgaged house has been elevated to a new position. Instead of a two-story with an overgrown lawn, it is an Estate. Even my debts have become nobler. They are no longer just bills; they are now Encumbrances. It's a fitting name, since apparently, even if I die, they get passed along to my heirs.

Other aspects of inheritances are not so simple. In the Will and Testament world, every bequeath, no matter how small, requires a translator. It would be impossible to simply say that I would like my favorite teacup to go to my daughter. This type of request would require an official memorandum directing my Executor to properly dispose of any portion of my personal and household effects according to Article 2 and subject to probate. After all, should anyone contest the teacup issue, it must be able to stand up under judicial scrutiny.

Which brings me to my favorite part of the Will. According to Article 9, "if any beneficiary shall contest the validity of the Will, then all benefits provided for such beneficiary are revoked." In other words, "Don't argue with your mother." You've got to love a document that gives you the last word even from the grave.

Other aspects of making out my Will were not so pleasant. Executor and I had to discuss the possibility that we might both perish at the same time. That eventuality would leave little Beneficiaries 1, 2, and 3 in need of a guardian. You can imagine the lively discussion this generated. Would we send them to his family or mine? To a city relative or a country one? To the most financially or the most spiritually stable? To our first choice or the kids' first choice? Fortunately, our interplanetary minds happen to be on the same wavelength, and we settled that matter, keeping our happy marriage intact.

The real dilemma came when we had to decide at what age the children would gain control of their inheritance—like the debt, the dog, and the change under the couch cushions. We felt sure that our oldest would be more than responsible by age twenty-two. And our youngest child certainly wasn't a concern. She could manage it all now. The question was what to do with our proverbial party boy—the middle child. He has lost his wallet a dozen times this year; he impulse-buys anything from sticky tack to dental floss; and he has made some bad investments in the form of unsecured loans to his mother. It is certainly enough to give us pause. Still, in the cause of fairness, we have resolved that each of them will share equally in a secured inheritance, such as it is.

What a comfort to know that you and I can also have the promise of a secured inheritance, and it, too, is fairly distributed to all who are in the family.

Yet to all who received [Christ], to those who believed in his name, he gave the right to become children of God—children born not of natural descent, nor of human decision, ... but born of God.

JOHN 1:12-13

So you are no longer a slave, but a son; and since you are a son, God has made you also an heir.

GALATIANS 4:7

How wonderfully uncomplicated—no Articles, Memorandums, or Executors, just simple faith in the Son of God, which "qualif[ies] us to share in the inheritance of the saints in light" (Col 1:12, NASB).

God has not bequeathed us "treasures on earth, where moth and rust destroy" (Mt 6:19), but instead has secured for us eternal life. Yet, as if that were not enough, He has also promised, "No mind has conceived what God has prepared for those who love him" (1 Cor 2:9) for those who have been renamed "sons of God."

It's settled. If I die tomorrow, an inheritance is secure for me.

Father in Heaven,
Thank You for adopting me into Your family and giving me the joy of call-ing You Abba, Daddy. Help me to keep my focus on the inheritance that is to come, not the possessions that I own. Remind me daily that nothing can compare to what You have prepared for me. Thank You that You have given it all freely through Jesus Christ because of Your great love for me.

What did God remind you of today?
Get a pencil and write it out.

Are You Talking to Me?

Logging the Miles   Today is _____

One word to describe my day would be _____

The greatest thing about today was _____
_____
_____
_____
_____
_____

The funniest thing that happened today was _____
_____
_____
_____
_____
_____

I was really frustrated by _____
_____
_____
_____
_____
_____

I wish I would have _____
_____
_____
_____
_____

Are You Talking to Me?
~~~~~~~

God, I could tell that You were with me today because _____

_____

_____

_____

_____

_____

_____

I'm ready to hear You speak, Lord. What I hear You say through it all is

_____

_____

_____

_____

_____

_____

God, because I heard You, I know that I should _____

_____

_____

_____

_____

_____

_____

A scripture that comes to mind is _____

_____

_____

_____

_____

_____

Day 3
Mirror, Mirror

When my son found out that I had become a certified personality trainer, he commissioned me right away to train his little brother, noting that he could use a new personality. You can imagine his disappointment when I explained that I don't give out personalities, I just identify them. There was no better place to start than in my own home. So, with questionnaires in hand, we set out to create a personality profile of our family.

My oldest son was the most eager to find out which of the four basic personalities was his. Would Chase be a perfect melancholy, driven by the need for perfection? That was ruled out with one look at his room. What about the powerful choleric, who likes to take charge of every situation? That would entail too much conflict for him. Maybe the fun-loving and popular sanguine, who is always the life of the party? Definitely too happy.

Chase is a peaceful phlegmatic, the all-purpose personality that never rocks the boat. Of course, that is mainly because rocking the boat would require too much energy, and phlegmatics are known to have a lazy streak.

This news didn't disturb Chase in the least. On the contrary, he felt vindicated. From his lounging position on the couch he said, "See, Mom, it's not my fault I'm so lazy. I was born that way. You'll just have to get used to it."

I had hoped he would see laziness as something to overcome, not his greatest virtue. Instead, he has adopted the phlegmatic mantra—that is, "Why stand when you can sit, why sit when you can lie down?"—as his new philosophy of life.

His younger brother never sits down. The energy around him is tangible, and he is always in motion. Unfortunately, he is never very productive. That's because Bailey is a sanguine. He uses every bit of vigor looking for fun. (And what could be more fun than finding out your personality?)

He skipped from room to room, singing, "I'm a penguin. I'm a penguin."

"Not a penguin, honey. You're a sanguine," I told him, but he was having too much fun to care about the details.

So I turned my attention to my daughter, who was impatiently waiting to hear about her personality. "Hannah, you are a choleric," I said without a doubt.

"What does that mean?" she asked.

"Well, cholerics are people who are hard workers. They like to be in charge because they can get things done quickly. But," I cautioned, "they can also be a little bossy, and they usually think they are right about everything."

In perfect form, she put her hands on her hips and said, "I am not bossy. I help people."

I could sympathize fully with her frustration. Like Hannah, I have a lot of choleric in me. So I could speak without judging when I told her, "It's just that not everyone wants our help." I could see this came as a total surprise to her. Who wouldn't want our help?

My husband was the last to get his new label. There is no question that, like Bailey, he is a fun-loving penguin—I mean sanguine. He enjoys life and doesn't sweat the details. After all, that's the job of the melancholy personalities. They are great with details, numbers, and schedules and at keeping the rest of us in line.

Unfortunately, there isn't an ounce of melancholy in our family, so there are certain areas where we are deficient. We all have a hard time finishing projects. We are terrible with budgets. We are rarely on time, and we could all use some practice in the area of sensitivity.

I am comforted in our lack, however, by the knowledge that everyone falls short somewhere. We all have strengths, to be sure, but we also have innate weaknesses. As much as we would like to have the strengths of all of the personality types and the weakness of none, only Jesus Christ fits that description.

> He [alone] is the image of the invisible God, the firstborn of all creation.... For in Christ all the fullness of the Deity lives in bodily form.
>
> COLOSSIANS 1:15; 2:9

Yet, lest we think, like Chase, that our inborn weakness give us an excuse, we must read on.

> And you have been given fullness in Christ.... Put to death, therefore, whatever belongs to your earthly nature.... You used to walk in these ways in the life you once lived. But now you must rid yourselves of all such things.... Put on the new self, which is being renewed in knowledge in the image of its Creator.
>
> COLOSSIANS 2:10; 3:4, 7, 8, 10

Jesus Christ is the ultimate personality trainer, and He is willing to transform our personalities into His image.

Dear Lord,
Thank you for creating me with a unique personality. Help me see myself as others see me and as I really am. Give me the wisdom to use my

strengths to serve You and the humility to allow You to work on my weaknesses. Transform me in the image of Your Son.

Where did you see God today?
Get a pencil and write it down.

Logging the Miles   Today is _____

One word to describe my day would be _____

The greatest thing about today was _____

_____

_____

_____

_____

_____

The funniest thing that happened today was _____

_____

_____

_____

_____

_____

I was really frustrated by _____

_____

_____

_____

_____

_____

I wish I would have _____

_____

_____

_____

_____

God, I could tell that You were with me today because _____

_____

_____

_____

_____

_____

I'm ready to hear You speak, Lord. What I hear You say through it all is

_____

_____

_____

_____

_____

God, because I heard You, I know that I should _____

_____

_____

_____

_____

A scripture that comes to mind is _____

_____

_____

_____

_____

Day 4
20/20/Not

For many years I have gotten a good giggle from my mother's struggle with her reading glasses. They are a joy to her, because they enable her to see, yet they also are a scourge, because she can never find them, even when they are on top of her head. Teasing her about the situation has provided many moments of jocularity for our family. It never occurred to me, however, that one day all of that amusement would focus on me.

Two years ago I began having headaches almost daily. Since I have a strong constitution, I knew that something out of the ordinary was afoot. Through self-diagnosis, I determined I was suffering from the effects of excessive caffeine, so I cut out the sodas, coffee, and chocolate that had previously made up 50 percent of my daily dietary intake. Thinking this "cold turkey" method would free me from the ills of artificial stimulants, I looked forward to being "clean" for the first time.

So much for healthy living! Not only did my headaches worsen, a feeling of lethargy also beset me. My usual get-up-and-go got up and went. It took less than a week to realize the problem was not caffeine. As I grabbed a Coke and a candy bar, I wondered what else it could be.

I decided that I should make an appointment to see a doctor. After all, it might be something serious, like an aneurysm or a brain tumor. I wondered if they would need to perform a CAT scan or possibly one of those tests where they attach dozens of electrodes to one's head to measure brain activity. Realizing how sick I might be,

I didn't delay in reaching for the phone book.

As I thumbed through the pages I noticed that I was squinting to make out the names. Instinctively, I held the phone book at arm's length, and the names became clear. For a split second I wondered what dreaded disease could not only cause my head such pain but also threaten to strike me blind. Then I realized that the more I squinted, the more my head ached.

A trip to the eye doctor, instead of the neurosurgeon, confirmed my new suspicion. I wasn't dying. I needed glasses. Relieved that my life had been spared, I prepared for a different kind of suffering. The day I arrived home with my drugstore reading glasses, I became my mother.

"I'll be happy to look at your homework. Has anybody seen my glasses?"

Now the jokes are at my expense, even though I have explained that it is unreasonable to expect me to find my glasses without having glasses with which to look. This kind of logical excuse has done nothing to appease my family's amusement.

"Mom, do you want us to call the nursing home now? They have nice people there who will read to you."

In an effort to appear less senile, I have purchased five pairs of glasses and strategically placed them around the house. The odds have greatly improved that I will locate a pair when I need them. Now my family just laughs at the way I wear my glasses, perched on the end of my nose. My only consolation is that this year reading glasses were also prescribed for my husband.

For all of us, a greater handicap than being physically sight-challenged is being spiritually sight-impaired. Jesus warned his disciples about this after teaching a parable to the multitudes that they did not fully understand.

Therefore I speak to them in parables; because while seeing, they do not see, and while hearing they do not hear, nor do they understand.... For the heart of this people has become dull ... and they have closed their eyes lest they should see with their eyes.

MATTHEW 13:13, 15, NASB

The prescription for this kind of blindness is a comprehensive treatment:

Do your best to add these things to your lives: to your faith, add goodness; and to your goodness, add knowledge; and to your knowledge, add self-control; and to your self-control, add patience; and to your patience, add service for God; and to your service for God, add kindness for your brothers and sisters in Christ; and to this kindness, add love. If all these things are in you and are growing, they will help you to be useful and productive in your knowledge of our Lord Jesus Christ. But anyone who does not have these things cannot see clearly. He is blind and has forgotten that he was made clean from his past sins.

2 PETER 1:5-9, NCV

If your spiritual sight has become a little blurry, slip on these attributes and see how they bring abundant life into focus.

God,
Thank You that You have given me the ability to see clearly the truths from Your Word. Forgive me for the times when my heart has been dull and I would not see things Your way. Keep my focus sharp by growing in me a heart of faith, goodness, knowledge, self-discipline, patience, service,

kindness, and love. Make me ever mindful of the great debt that You have cancelled for me.

What did you hear God say today?
Get a pencil and write it down.

Logging the Miles   Today is _____

One word to describe my day would be _____

The greatest thing about today was _____

_____

_____

_____

_____

_____

The funniest thing that happened today was _____

_____

_____

_____

_____

_____

I was really frustrated by _____

_____

_____

_____

_____

_____

31

Are You Talking to Me?

~~~~~~

I wish I would have _____

_____

_____

_____

_____

God, I could tell that You were with me today because _____

_____

_____

_____

_____

_____

I'm ready to hear You speak, Lord. What I hear You say through it all is

_____

_____

_____

_____

_____

God, because I heard You, I know that I should _____

_____

_____

_____

_____

A scripture that comes to mind is _____

_____

_____

_____

_____

Day 5
Mauve Madness

aking room in a busy family schedule for one-on-one time can be a challenge, so I was thrilled when my then seven-year-old daughter cleared her schedule for me. This was not an easy trick, considering her pressing daily itinerary.

Besides her regular obligation at school, she usually has two or three social commitments a week, such as a birthday party, a sleep-over, or lunch with friends. Then her afternoons are filled with the really serious pursuits.

Once a week she dons her jodhpurs for horseback riding lessons, and twice a week she slips into a jersey for baseball practice. The latter keeps her in prime shape for the weekend game. Being the only girl on the team may have its advantages, like learning to spit and being the only one who is still cute when she strikes out, but it also has its burdens. It takes extra effort to get the respect of all those seasoned first-grade boys.

That's why it was a real sacrifice on her part to skip two games to spend the weekend with me. I, on the other hand, didn't have anything that conflicted with the upcoming mother-daughter conference, so we made plans to attend.

During the conference, we were given several hours of free time and a host of activities from which to choose. Among the least tempting were the tea party, card embossing, and crafts. In my opinion, if you really want to punish prisoners, don't send them to solitary confinement. Just send them to craft-making.

We opted for horseback riding and canoeing. Both of these gave us a chance to be alone and just talk. Not once was I interrupted by a phone call, nor did cartoons distract her.

On the way back to the cabin, we inadvertently passed the craft cottage. There were several mother-daughter pairs gluing buttons, painting treasure boxes, and sprinkling glitter. Just as I was about to make one of those gag-me-with-a-spoon motions, I noticed Hannah admiring all the doodads being produced.

Against my better judgment I asked, "You don't want to make a craft, do you?"

"No, that's OK. You don't really want to," she said.

I swallowed hard. "I want to do whatever you want to do."

"Well, it might be fun to make one of those star door hangers," she said hopefully.

"I think we should," I said with false conviction. "We could probably knock one out in half an hour."

For the next three hours we splatter-painted, hot-glued, and arranged flowers. I even caught myself mixing paint to get the perfect shade of mauve. Eventually we left the craft cottage with the most incredibly perfect door hanger ever created. With just a little guidance from me, some of it even helpful, Hannah planned, organized, and produced a very tasteful ornament.

We finished just in time for memento pictures by the lake. Since the photographer was late, the girls played outdoor ping-pong while the moms enjoyed the breeze on the deck. Forty-five minutes later the photographer finally arrived. Just at that moment I heard a splash, followed by hysterical laughter. Hannah, dressed and ready for the picture, had fallen in the lake. The good news was that she had saved the Ping-Pong ball she was diving after.

The photographer snapped a picture as I pulled her out of the water, dripping from head to toe. It wasn't the pose I had planned on, but the moment she captured is one of our favorite memories.

It comes just behind craft making.

The finale to the weekend came when we filled the bathtub full of frogs to surprise one of the moms who always takes a late-night bath. When she pushed open the shower curtain, wearing nothing but a smile, fifteen frogs stared back at her. As she came flying out of the bathroom, we serenaded her with "Jeremiah Was a Bullfrog." She was definitely surprised.

Yet not as surprised as I continue to be at how stealthily time robs the opportunity for making such special memories. It seems like just yesterday I was walking hand in hand through the zoo with my own mom, agreeing that the otter was my favorite animal, too.

Fortunately, the One who created time is also the One who can help us capture it. "There is a time for everything, and a season for every activity under heaven" (Eccl 3:1). Whether we are coming into the world or leaving it, weeping or laughing, making memories or remembering them, God has appointed the times of our lives. We need only discover, accept, and appreciate what each one has to offer, before the moment slips away.

The seasons may come and go faster than we like, but they are never too short or too long for those taking advantage of God-given opportunities in the midst of their pressing daily itineraries.

Dear Lord,

I realize that the twenty-four hours in each of my days are a gift from You. Help me to use them wisely. Give me eyes to see the divine opportunities You provide to invest in relationships with the people I love. Help me to discern the urgent from the important.

Are You Talking to Me?

Were you listening for God in your day? What did He say? Write it down.

Logging the Miles   Today is _____

One word to describe my day would be _____

The greatest thing about today was _____

_____

_____

_____

_____

The funniest thing that happened today was _____

_____

_____

_____

_____

I was really frustrated by _____

_____

_____

_____

_____

I wish I would have _____

_____

_____

_____

_____

Are You Talking to Me?

God, I could tell that You were with me today because _____

_____

_____

_____

_____

_____

_____

I'm ready to hear You speak, Lord. What I hear You say through it all is

_____

_____

_____

_____

_____

_____

God, because I heard You, I know that I should _____

_____

_____

_____

_____

_____

A scripture that comes to mind is _____

_____

_____

_____

_____

_____

Day 6
Compu-cide

Whoever said that you should make lemonade when life gives you lemons did not buy his computer at the same place we did. If he had, his motto would have been, "When life gives you lemons, get a lawyer." The day finally came when I found myself pulling out that desperate phrase, "Well, I've got this lawyer friend ..."

The whole ugly business began when we purchased a new computer. Being techno-illiterate, I wasn't consulted on the details. When my husband said we were getting sixty-four rams, I wondered how we would keep them out of the neighbor's yard. With no help from me, he purchased a state-of-the-art PC that he was sure would replace the dog in our affections.

For the first few days he and the kids never came out of the study. When I was eventually given a turn, I was determined to show it who was boss. Within an hour it refused to load my programs. Though I think it smelled fear, the service technician said it had a faulty CD drive.

It took three months for the new part to arrive from Oklahoma City. I'm not sure, but I think it took a detour in Tulsa. I called regularly to see if they had traced our wayward part. No one knew anything, so we just waited. At last the new part arrived and we were fully operational—for about two months.

That's how long it took before the computer froze and refused even to let us turn it off. The only way to regain control was to unplug the power. Again a technician was dispatched to diagnose the possessed processor, though an exorcist might have been more helpful. I fully expected to enter the study and find it spewing green goo and screeching "fatal error, fatal eeeerrrroooorrr."

Once its demons had been exorcised, the computer once again could take instructions from us, but this was more than the PC could bear. We found it one morning, totally unresponsive, the cord wrapped around its monitor, a clear case of compu-cide. The autopsy revealed a fried motherboard.

Apparently, though, computers, like cats, have multiple lives. A few new parts, and we were told it was as good as new. (Not a comforting thought.) And then a few more parts and a few more, until last month we said, "No more! Give us a new computer."

Not surprisingly, the company no longer manufactures the exact model we purchased. We were surprised, however, when they offered to replace ours with one worth half the value. No matter how we pleaded our case, it fell on deaf ears—that is, until I mentioned "this lawyer friend."

Suddenly we had someone's attention, but it wasn't the type we had hoped to get. A store employee who took charge offered his unsolicited advice about attorneys, badgered me in a store full of customers, and told me we could take his offer or leave it, it was all we were going to get.

"And what was your name, sir?" I inquired through a strained smile and gritted teeth.

I took his name and made a call to another store in the chain. I planned to start my crusade against this injustice by filing an official complaint. Then I'd hire my lawyer friend. It was clear I was getting nowhere on my own.

When I finally reached a manager, he wanted to know the whole story. So I told him about the runaway CD drive, the green goo, the motherboard fiasco, and the scandalous way I had been treated.

After listening he said, "Why don't you let me see if I can help you? I'll track down the service records and then call the warranty company."

From that moment on, Mike became our advocate. He asked us what our computer needs were and found a machine that was superior to the one that had crashed, yet no more expensive. He called to keep us informed, and when the warranty company balked, he interceded with them to get what he thought was best for us. Thanks to his intercession, my husband is once again in the study, herding the new rams.

Sometimes, the best we can do is put ourselves into someone else's hands, someone who can do what we can't.

> Christ Jesus is He who died, yes, rather who was raised, who is at the right hand of God, who also intercedes for us.
>
> ROMANS 8:34, NASB

He is the defender of the defenseless, the mediator between God and man, the One who forever represents us. Through Him we have direct access to God, because "we have an advocate with the Father, Jesus Christ the righteous" (1 Jn 2:1, NASB).

When Jesus Christ pleads our case, victory is assured. No defense attorney alive can represent us the way that He does.

Dear Jesus,

Thank You for continuing to intercede for me. I trust You to be my advocate. I know that in all things You are able to defend me, deliver me, protect me, and guide me. Even when my reputation is at stake, I know I can trust You to undertake my battles. I'd like to talk to You now about some things I have been trying to fix myself.

Are You Talking to Me?
~~~~~~~~

Was God trying to reach you today?
If you heard Him, write about it.

Logging the Miles   Today is _____

One word to describe my day would be _____

The greatest thing about today was _____
_____
_____
_____
_____

The funniest thing that happened today was _____
_____
_____
_____
_____

I was really frustrated by _____
_____
_____
_____
_____

I wish I would have _____
_____
_____
_____
_____

Are You Talking to Me?
~~~~~~~~

God, I could tell that You were with me today because _____

_____

_____

_____

_____

_____

_____

I'm ready to hear You speak, Lord. What I hear You say through it all is

_____

_____

_____

_____

_____

_____

God, because I heard You, I know that I should _____

_____

_____

_____

_____

_____

A scripture that comes to mind is _____

_____

_____

_____

_____

_____

Day 7

Size 12DD

My shoes may be only a size seven, but there is no way my son is ready to fill them. Still, what fun I have watching him try.

When he was eleven, Chase began looking for ways to make some extra money so he could buy paintball equipment that his dad and I refused to furnish. First, he tried asking us to raise his allowance, but when that elicited nothing but a laugh, he realized he would have to actually earn the money himself.

"How much do you think I could get for my Lego collection?" he asked.

"Let's see. You have $350 worth of Legos. On the open garage sale market," I guessed, "about $15."

"That stinks," he complained. Yet what could I say? When it comes to used Legos, it's a buyer's market. "I guess I'll have to get a job," he concluded.

After two weeks of unsuccessful job-hunting, he was ready to give up on finding an adolescent vocation. Then a friend offered him his first baby-sitting job. I was surprised at how quickly he accepted, considering how much he grumbles when it comes to watching his brother and sister. However, with money to be made, he eagerly agreed.

In preparation for the job, he grilled me with questions like "What should I do with him?" "What do I do if he gets sick?" and the all-important "How much should I charge?"

We talked through all of his concerns, then I assured him that

$10 an hour was not the going rate for baby-sitters. I suggested that he let my friend decide the wage.

When the big day finally arrived, Chase woke up ready to go. He was like a changed boy, the weight of his responsibility transforming him. I took the opportunity to give him some last-minute instructions.

"Remember, you're there to keep Wilson entertained. Do the things he enjoys, and follow all of their house rules. Make sure he picks up his toys, and don't leave any dirty dishes. Mrs. Hinze should come home to find a house as clean as the one she left." He listened intently.

"You know, I might even wash her dishes and take out her trash," he said.

Incredibly, these are the same chores he avoids at all cost at home. Still, I was glad to see that he got the point. I knew, at the very least, that the house would be safe from ruin. Beyond that I wasn't sure, so I prayed.

Two hours into the baby-sitting job, I called to see how things were going. "Everything is fine, Mom," he reported. "But I can't talk. Wilson and I are playing pool."

Around noon Chase dragged in with a generous amount of hard-earned cash in his pocket. He was exhausted, and he immediately retreated to the couch for a nap. When I questioned what could have made him so tired, he looked incredulous.

"Mom, you just don't understand what it's like to take care of someone for four straight hours."

Did I dare jump on that line? Of course. "Honey, I take care of three of you twenty-four hours a day, every day of the year. I think I might have a little idea what it's like."

"That's not the same. I had to do everything with him. We picked blackberries, played Nintendo, went for a walk, and watched some TV. It was hard work. I had to be like his parent."

He was much too serious for me to diminish the significance of the task he had accomplished. Though I do the same thing hundredfold every day, he could not imagine that I understood the emotional and physical stamina it took for him to carry that burden for just four hours.

How often I hold the same mistaken assumption about God. "Lord, I am so tired. I have been doing this very difficult thing, and You just don't understand what it's like."

Yet God answers us as He answered Job, lovingly reminding us that He does understand, because the weight He carries is far greater than anything we can imagine.

Where were you when I laid the earth's foundation?... Have you ever given orders to the morning, or shown the dawn its place?... Have you journeyed to the springs of the sea or walked in the recesses of the deep?... Have you seen the gates of the shadow of death?... Would you discredit my justice?

JOB 38:4; 12, 16, 17; 40:8

Oh, that I might learn to answer like Job: "I know that you can do all things, no plan of yours can be thwarted.... Surely I spoke of things I did not understand, things too wonderful for me to know" (Job 42:2, 3).

But God does know, and He invites us to bring our greatest burdens to Him.

Come to me, all you who are weary and burdened and I will give you rest. Take my yoke upon you and learn from me, for I am gentle and humble in heart, and you will find rest for your souls.

MATTHEW 11:28-29

I cannot walk in God's shoes, but I can certainly stay on the same path, knowing that whether it's rocky or smooth, He has gone there before me and made the way passable and given my soul rest.

Dear Lord,
Some days I feel as if no one understands all the burdens I carry. I get overwhelmed with the responsibilities. Help me to see that You are going before me, and help me to trust that You do understand. Give me strength when I am weary, and give me faith when I am weak. Thank You that I never have to walk the rocky paths alone.

In what ways did God walk with you today?
Write them down.

Logging the Miles   Today is _____

One word to describe my day would be _____

The greatest thing about today was _____

_____

_____

_____

_____

The funniest thing that happened today was _____

_____

_____

_____

_____

Are You Talking to Me?
~~~~~~~

I was really frustrated by _____

_____

_____

_____

I wish I would have _____

_____

_____

_____

God, I could tell that You were with me today because _____

_____

_____

_____

I'm ready to hear You speak, Lord. What I hear You say through it all is

_____

_____

_____

_____

God, because I heard You, I know that I should _____

_____

_____

_____

A scripture that comes to mind is _____

_____

_____

_____

47

Day 8
You're Outta Here

e arrived at our house one evening about nine o'clock. With an inviting smile and a heavy Spanish accent, he extended his hand and said, "I am Caleb."

It was the moment the kids had been waiting for. They had been counting the days since we had volunteered to host the foreigner coming for our church's missions conference. Finally, there he stood, as we greeted him eagerly and bombarded him with questions.

"Where are you from? Do you have any kids? Do you like dogs?"

Caleb, still perfecting his English, understood us as long as we talked slowly. My husband, however, also added volume, a Spanish accent, and a few Spanish words. Being from El Paso, he felt it was a good opportunity to brush up on his second language.

Loudly he said things like, "Our niños just got to our casa from playing bas-a-ball" (somehow an Italian accent slipped in), and, "We have two perros (dogs), three gatos (cats), but no cabritos (goats)." (I think goat just happened to be in his vocabulary.)

I chose to employ the more subtle means of sign language. Like a bizarre game of charades, Caleb worked to decipher my too-quick English and flailing hand motions. He, on the other hand, more relaxed, communicated competently, his frequent misuse of verb tenses endearing him to us.

All of this seemed to entertain Caleb immensely. Soon he was correcting Tony's Spanish and telling the kids all about his life in South America.

Caleb had been a lawyer in Bolivia before committing his life to

48

Christ five years earlier. It was then that he felt a call to preach the gospel. He shared Christ with the Indian workers in the cocaine fields of Bolivia until God led him to seminary in South Texas, from which he had just graduated.

Yet, for all his education, we discovered there was one thing about which Caleb knew nothing—baseball. The next day, with a whiffle ball and paper plates for bases, the kids taught Caleb America's favorite pastime. For an hour, our backyard was Spring Training Camp. It was kids versus adults, and Caleb was rookie of the year. He pitched, hit a home run, and even umpired, calling out with an accent, "Striking Three! You are out of there!"

Though he had a great time, we were certain baseball was not his calling. His was to the Great Commission. While he had intended to return to the Indians in South America, God had instead opened the door for him to begin a mission in the Rio Grande Valley, his monthly support being less than one of our monthly car payments. Yet, with few possessions and even fewer resources, he seemed certain God would provide everything he needed to accomplish His work.

After all, that's what God specializes in: providing in unexpected ways. For example, none of us expected what God would provide even while Caleb stayed with us. Out of the blue it occurred to Tony that he had several business suits that no longer fit and that, if altered, might work for Caleb as he began his ministry. My husband was also surprised to find belts, jeans, and new shoes he couldn't wear. But God was not surprised.

Each thing fit Caleb as if it had been tailor-made just for him, and we realized that God had had it planned all along. Who would have thought that a lawyer from Bolivia would be wearing my husband's suits as he preached the gospel to Mexican immigrants in South Texas? Only God.

With tears of thanksgiving, Caleb praised God and thanked us. We were thankful, too, that in His mercy, God did not let us miss "the privilege of sharing in this service to the saints" (2 Cor 8:4). Though a small thing in our estimation, God made it a holy calling.

> Dear friend, you are faithful in what you are doing for the brothers, even though they are strangers to you.... You will do well to send them on their way in a manner worthy of God. It was for the sake of the Name that they went out, receiving no help from the pagans. We ought therefore to show hospitality to such men so that we may *work together* for the truth.
>
> 3 JOHN 5-8, *emphasis added*

Even more amazing, Paul clarifies that there is great blessing in giving, not just in going:

> You sent me aid again and again when I was in need. Not that I am looking for a gift, but I am looking for what may be credited to your account.... Your gifts are a fragrant offering, an acceptable sacrifice, pleasing to God.
>
> PHILIPPIANS 4:16-18

It is God's hand that is extended to both the sender and the worker, inviting each one to join in His harvest, working together to share the truth.

Dear Lord,
Thank You for the workers that You have sent into the harvest, and thank You for the senders. Give me clear direction on the part You would have me play in fulfilling the Great Commission. Grant me opportuni-

ties to share in the service to the saints, to meet the needs of those You have called, and to extend hospitality to Your servants. Show me the things that will be an acceptable sacrifice that is pleasing to You.

What did God show you today?

Logging the Miles   Today is _____

One word to describe my day would be _____

The greatest thing about today was _____

_____

_____

_____

_____

_____

The funniest thing that happened today was _____

_____

_____

_____

_____

_____

I was really frustrated by _____

_____

_____

_____

_____

_____

Are You Talking to Me?

I wish I would have _____

_____

_____

_____

_____

God, I could tell that You were with me today because _____

_____

_____

_____

_____

I'm ready to hear You speak, Lord. What I hear You say through it all is

_____

_____

_____

_____

_____

God, because I heard You, I know that I should _____

_____

_____

_____

_____

A scripture that comes to mind is _____

_____

_____

_____

_____

Day 9
Super Granny

I couldn't believe it. The kids were at camp, and in the middle of a very busy summer, I had a whole week to myself.

It felt like the old days. I was cruising down the open road, alone and for the moment with no responsibilities. I almost felt eighteen again, or at least I would have, had I not been driving the family minivan with Barney lying on the floorboard. Still, with oldies playing on the radio, I was headed back to the rural Oklahoma town where I had spent so many teenage summers with my grandmother. As I wound my way on the familiar streets of Blackwell, everything dripped with nostalgia, and I found myself longing for the good old days. Just as in the past, I was sure on this summer day Grandma would be waiting to welcome me with arms open wide and something special baking in the oven.

I could hardly wait to wrap my arms around her. I was sure she, too, was counting the minutes. I honked enthusiastically as I parked the car and was surprised when she didn't immediately appear. I rang the bell and waited, and then rang again. Eventually the door opened wide, and I was finally in the arms of my grandmother. That one hug was the last familiar thing that happened during my visit.

First, there were no goodies in the oven as I had expected. Instead it was leftovers, Sonic Burgers, and Kentucky Fried Chicken while I was there. Frankly, my eighty-year-old grandmother was just too busy to cook. She was in the middle of remodeling her house. Her days were spent painting, wallpapering, and moving furniture. "Surely, Grandma, you're not doing this alone," I protested.

"Oh no, Dearie," she replied, "Aunt Betty is helping me." Betty was seventy-five.

Because the days were full with her comings and goings, I was determined not to wear her out by staying up late. I was in bed each night by eleven. She never came to bed before two in the morning. On the second night, she didn't come to bed at all. "I wanted to get that freezer cleaned out," she explained. "I'll take a nap this morning." Who was this wonder woman in support hose? And where did she put my elderly grandmother?

Abounding energy wasn't the only phenomenon. What about this excitement she had for God's Word? I didn't remember her ever bubbling with excitement when she talked about Scripture, as she was now. Something was different. A Christian from a very young age, my grandmother had the privilege of being raised in a God-fearing home by parents who passed their faith to all nine of their children. In turn, she and my grandfather raised a family with faith at the center of their home. But what I was seeing was more than that. It was a seventy years in the making faith that suddenly seemed fresh. How could that be?

"Dearie," she explained, "when I was younger, no one told me to read the Bible for myself. I just believed, and I did what I knew was right. We listened to the preacher, and we did what he taught. They didn't teach you about the Bible, like they do today, to read it for yourself."

She continued, "I'm finally understanding things I never did before. I'm seeing it for myself, and there is no end to the things God is showing me. I'm growing like never before."

Didn't the apostle Peter say something like that?

Like newborn babes, long for the pure milk of the word, that by it you may grow [even when you are eighty] in respect to salvation.

1 PETER 2:2, NASB

54

With a faith nearly seventy years old, that is what my grandmother is doing. With the freshness of a newborn babe, she is drinking the Word for herself. Her obedience no longer hinges on the do's and don'ts espoused from a pulpit but is instead given in genuine response to time spent alone with her own Father. "The old things have passed away, behold new things have comee" (2 Cor 5:17, NASB). Indeed, this was my grandmother, being made new in a myriad of ways.

The good old days for her are probably just as precious as they are to me, but I'll take my cue from Grandma and keep moving forward with God.

Lord,
How I pray that you will make my faith fresh. Remind me again of those things that You and You alone provide. Take me down the paths where I can learn new things about You and learn to trust You in new ways. Thrill me with Your presence, Lord, all the days of my life.

What was this day of your life like?
Get your pencil and write it down.

Logging the Miles   Today is _____

One word to describe my day would be _____

The greatest thing about today was _____

_____

_____

_____

_____

Are You Talking to Me?

The funniest thing that happened today was _____

_____

_____

_____

_____

_____

_____

I was really frustrated by _____

_____

_____

_____

_____

_____

_____

I wish I would have _____

_____

_____

_____

_____

_____

God, I could tell that You were with me today because _____

_____

_____

_____

_____

_____

_____

Are You Talking to Me?
~~~~~~~~

I'm ready to hear You speak, Lord. What I hear You say through it all is

_____

_____

_____

_____

_____

_____

_____

_____

_____

_____

God, because I heard You, I know that I should _____

_____

_____

_____

_____

_____

_____

_____

_____

A scripture that comes to mind is _____

_____

_____

_____

_____

_____

_____

Day 10
Thanks for Nothing

There are two things you should never put off—changing the cat litter and car maintenance. One I do faithfully; the other I learned the hard way.

One day I noticed a residue under my car. So I asked about it when I had the oil changed. "You're leaking transmission fluid," the mechanic diagnosed. "You need to take it to your dealership."

Since he assured me it was safe to drive, however, I decided to put it off until I could go a day without the car. Months passed, and that day never came. In fact, if anything, the demands on my taxi service grew.

The problem peaked when I committed to ferrying five fifth-grade girls to a science camp. On the way to pick them up, I noticed my car was a little sluggish slipping into gear. "That's odd," I thought, but since it wasn't affecting the forward momentum of the car, we headed down the road as planned.

When I got home, common sense got the better of me, and before I made the return trip to get the girls, I had the transmission checked. I dropped the car at the dealership service department and told them I had to have it back the next day.

The service manager called later, explaining that they had pulled the transmission out of my car and it would be days before I saw it again. Knowing my situation, he was holding a loaner van at the rental desk for me. This, however, was news to the rental agent when I arrived to pick it up. "I already have it booked for the weekend," the young man explained as he paged through his logs.

"Well, I have to have a van, or five girls get stuck at camp," I countered. "What if I take the van now, pick up the girls, and bring it back this afternoon? Then you can have the van and give me something different."

This plan seemed to make everyone happy, temporarily. After I returned the girls safely to their parents, I rushed the van back to the rental counter. Thinking I was doing them a favor by wasting no time, I bristled when the rental agent pointed out that I had forgotten to refill the gas tank. Then, adding insult to injury, he started the paperwork on a subcompact.

"It's the only thing we have left to loan," he assured me.

On my way out to refill the van with gas, I stopped at the service counter to see how the work on my own car was progressing. I said something like, "There is no way we can drive a dinky subcompact for more than a day. When will my car be ready?"

A smiling woman opened the service log and said, "Didn't we say Tuesday?"

"I was hoping they had made more progress today than expected," I said, without humor.

"Well, the transmission man is off today because he works on Saturdays."

"Today is Friday," I deduced, "so he will work on it tomorrow."

"No, he worked last Saturday, so he is off this Saturday."

I recapped, "So my car has been sitting in the back since Thursday with no transmission, and no one is going to work on it until Monday?"

"Yes, but it is the first thing on his schedule."

It was clear that I would be in the Matchbox car for more than a day. I glanced toward the rental desk and said flatly, "Could you have the white car ready to go when I get back from the gas station?"

It was ready, so the kids transferred all their backpacks, GameBoys, and empty French fry containers out of the van and into our phone booth on wheels for the ten-minute drive home.

By the time we pulled into the driveway, my breathing had returned to normal and my frustrations had begun to ebb. Now what flooded my thoughts were echoes of the arrogant tone I had used, impatiently trying to get my way.

I could also hear the much gentler voice of God's convicting spirit: "Kim, you are 'to be ready to do whatever is good; to slander no one; to be peaceable and considerate, and to show true humility toward all men' (Ti 3:1-2), 'giving no cause for offense in anything in order that the ministry not be disgraced' (2 Cor 6:3, NASB), 'making the most of the opportunity. Let your speech always be with grace ... so that you may know how you should respond to each person' (Col 4:6, NASB)."

Great. How do you respond with grace to folks you have just terrorized? There was only one way I could think of, by using that "true humility" we are called to—and a batch of chocolate chip cookies.

Drawing on the grace God promises to provide to the humble (see Jas 4:6), I made personal apologies to all of my victims when I finally picked up my car a few days later. With cookies in hand, I tried to make the most of the second opportunity God had graciously given me.

Now I am convinced that the two things you should never put off are a spirit of humility and an owed apology. Both require grace, and both are usually learned the hard way.

Dear Lord,
Please bring to my mind those times that I have offended others, have not been considerate or peaceable, or have slandered and lacked humility.

Are You Talking to Me?
~~~~~~~

Give me the grace to know how to respond to each person to whom I have given offense, that I might not disgrace Your name.

Is there something God brought to your mind today? Record it.

Logging the Miles   Today is _____

One word to describe my day would be _____

The greatest thing about today was _____
_____
_____
_____
_____
_____

The funniest thing that happened today was _____
_____
_____
_____
_____
_____

I was really frustrated by _____
_____
_____
_____
_____
_____

Are You Talking to Me?
~~~~~~~~

I wish I would have _____

_____

_____

_____

_____

God, I could tell that You were with me today because _____

_____

_____

_____

_____

_____

I'm ready to hear You speak, Lord. What I hear You say through it all is

_____

_____

_____

_____

_____

God, because I heard You, I know that I should _____

_____

_____

_____

_____

A scripture that comes to mind is _____

_____

_____

_____

_____

Day 11
Germ Warfare

It was crunch time. With just twelve hours before I was due to speak at a women's group, I decided it was time to get serious. So I locked myself in the study and began cranking out visuals and handouts.

A stranger peering in would have thought I was an organizational whiz. My family suspected an alien impostor had replaced me. A deadline was looming, however, so I was in high gear until 2 A.M. As I finally turned out the lights, crashing from the adrenaline rush, I heard little feet on the stairs. My only thought was, "Not tonight." Yet there stood Bailey, wide awake and green in the gills.

"I don't feel good, Mom." Then, with eight-year-old medical expertise, he told me his symptoms. "My stomach hurts, and my cheeks hurt. And I have a funny taste in my mouth. I tried to go back to sleep, but ..."

He was unable to finish his self-diagnosis because his head was in the toilet for the next ten minutes. He finally concluded, "I think I'm sick."

For an hour I escorted him back and forth to the bathroom. Finally I made the dreaded decision that he needed nausea medicine. "Sweetie, do you know what a suppository is?" Though it was unpleasant for him, I assured him it was no picnic for me, either. Yet that wasn't my biggest concern. For the boy who loves to entertain a crowd, I knew this would be new material for him in the lunchroom. I fell asleep imagining the look on his teacher's face when he shared the details.

Four hours later, with the sun coming up, his older brother casually mentioned, "I don't really feel well." I almost had him convinced it was his imagination when he, too, made a run for the bathroom. With just an hour before I was to speak and two sick kids, I decided to beg my sister to baby-sit her loving, slightly gross nephews. As I sent their little sister off to school, I gave the boys strict instructions not to infect their Aunt Tammi.

All went well during the presentation. The audience laughed at all the appropriate places, took notes, and asked questions. And the visuals looked even better at 9 A.M. than they had at 2 A.M. When I arrived home, my sister reported that the boys weren't better, but they weren't worse. She added, "I heard about the suppositories." Thirty minutes later my daughter came home from school with a stomachache.

They were still feeling puny the next morning, so I decided to let them all stay home again. I misjudged the situation. By noon they were sword fighting, and I realized I had made a mistake. So I fed them lunch and told them to use the extra energy to catch up on the chores they had missed.

"Chores? But we're sick," they moaned, as if in relapse.

"I'm afraid being sick of chores doesn't count. Get to work," I ordered. Even chores didn't wear them out, though. I decided to send them outside.

"Take your brother and sister and go for a bike ride," I told my oldest. "The fresh air will do you good."

They returned later, without Bailey. "Where is your brother?" I asked.

"Oh, he stopped at his teacher's house on the next street," they explained.

I could just hear the conversation. "No, I wasn't really sick today.

Do you know what a suppository is?" Short of a coma, I decided, they were never staying home again.

I hate to admit this, but during those three long days, the phrase "I decided" characterized all my actions. I decided when and how to work on my presentation. I decided what to do with the kids. I decided when to send them to school and what to do with them while they were home. I had decided I could handle the small crisis on my own. Yet, though my self-sufficiency got me smoothly through, that is all I got. I have to wonder now, what more could I have had?

> May the God of hope fill you with all joy and peace *as you trust in him,* so that you may overflow with hope by the power of the Holy Spirit.
>
> ROMANS 15:13, emphasis added

I cannot say that joy, peace, hope, or power overflowed in my life as I trusted in myself. I just felt relieved that the three days were over.

Looking back and sensing what I missed, I have decided one more thing. Next time I will come near to God, and He will come near to me. I will humble myself before the Lord, and He will lift me up (see Jas 4:10).

We will probably still have nausea, but I won't be sick at heart.

Dear Lord,
Forgive me for the times when I don't rely on You. Help me not to trust in my own strength but to look to You. Today show me how to come near to You in the midst of my daily problems. As I do, fill me with joy and peace so that I may overflow with the power of the Holy Spirit.

How did you rely on God today? Write about it.

Logging the Miles   Today is _____

One word to describe my day would be _____

The greatest thing about today was _____

_____

_____

_____

_____

_____

The funniest thing that happened today was _____

_____

_____

_____

_____

I was really frustrated by _____

_____

_____

_____

_____

I wish I would have _____

_____

_____

_____

_____

Are You Talking to Me?

God, I could tell that You were with me today because _____

_____

_____

_____

_____

_____

I'm ready to hear You speak, Lord. What I hear You say through it all is

_____

_____

_____

_____

_____

God, because I heard You, I know that I should _____

_____

_____

_____

_____

A scripture that comes to mind is _____

_____

_____

_____

_____

Day 12
Family Roots

If my life were a Broadway play, it would be *Hair*. The playbill would read: The story of individual freedom, self-discovery, and really cool hair. The cast would be my family, and the only thing missing would be the dance numbers—and we would, of course, wear our clothes.

The play opens after school one day when my son reminds me that it's time for haircuts: "Drop us at the mall and we'll get our hair cut while you pick Angela up at school," Chase suggests.

The scene cuts to the mall, where I ask, "Do you each know how you want your hair cut?"

My nephew, William, is very decisive. "Number two shave on the sides. Number four on top." I like a boy who knows his own hair. It shows bold confidence, if not cutting-edge style.

Chase isn't so self-assured, so the stylist recommends he look through some style books.

"Then I'll go next," Bailey offers. "I know exactly what I want. Long in the middle and short on the sides." With my eight-year-old climbing into the chair, I exit stage left with my daughter to pick up my niece from the high school.

When we return, fifteen minutes later, I am treated to a flash-back of what I have missed. Apparently, Bailey's idea of long hair in the middle was a Mohawk. The dialogue had gone like this:

"My mom said I could cut it like I wanted, remember?" Bailey debated.

"Well, I don't think that included a Mohawk," the stylist countered.

"But that's what I want, and the customer is always right," he reminded her.

"Not until the customer is twelve," she said.

He settled for a burr, but is hoping for a revised script.

Stage right, Chase is still considering his options. At twelve, I feel he is due a little more freedom of expression. "I want something that will look good bleached."

For the past month he had been trying to convince his dad that bleaching his hair is not a sign of anarchy, just taste. With a good report card in hand, he feels he has a little leverage. Now all he needs is a really cool haircut. At the end of the scene, he finally settles on a trendy spiked style.

Later that day: "When I was a kid," his dad comments, "stylists were called barbers, and they gave only flat tops." Then he hesitantly OKs the bleach job.

I have to admit, when I thought about having children, I always imagined it would be my daughter fussing about her hair. It never occurred to me that I would be bleaching my roots alongside my son.

As Scene 2 unfolds, I am a little nervous when I start working the highlighter through his hair. What if it looks as bad as the first perm my mom gave me? I guess he could always go with the Kojak look. Fortunately, my worries are in vain. Within an hour his hair is bleached and spiked into a very GQ do.

The next day, Scene 3, it's my turn. Not sure what I want, I give my hair care professional carte blanche. She decides I need short and straight. So she chops off my hair and irons it. I find this fascinating and much more fun than, say, ironing clothes. For the first time ever, I am on the cutting edge of vogue. I have to try this at home, so I run to the store to purchase my exciting new appliance.

First I iron my hair, and then I beg my daughter to let me try it out on her. Though she will have absolutely nothing to do with it, my teenage niece lets me experiment on her. Observing all the hoopla, my husband wonders why, if I find ironing so much fun, he has to press his own shirts.

"Honey, ironing shirts is about work. Ironing hair is about freedom of expression. Don't you see?"

He would be the first to admit, however, that our forms of individual expression are an absurdity to him. His idea of cutting edge is to shave his mustache. Still, he respects our right to be expressive, within reason (that is, no tattoos, body piercing, or clogs).

That is probably the moral of our hair drama; individual freedom tempered by reasonable boundaries ensures harmony. Could we have gotten that idea from Scripture?

It is for freedom that Christ has set us free. Stand firm, then, and do not let yourselves be burdened again by a yoke of slavery.

GALATIANS 5:1

Not only has God given us freedom from sin through Christ but also freedom from the constraints of a code or law that dictates our every move.

Instead, as Christians we are bound only by our commitment to serve and obey Christ and His Word and by our willingness to limit our liberty for the sake of another (see 1 Cor 10). Beyond that, God has "set [our] feet in a spacious place" (Ps 31:8), where we can play out our individuality and discover the joy of the unique roles God has given us. Though He directs, the scriptwriting is up to us.

Dear Lord,
Thank You for the freedom You give me in Christ. Help me not to abuse
those liberties by exercising them in a way that offends others around me.
Yet also help me not to impose my standards in a way that may cause oth-
ers to lose the freedom You have given them. Help me to judge my action
rightly as I serve and obey You.

Did God meet you somewhere today? Write about it.

Logging the Miles   Today is _____

One word to describe my day would be _____

The greatest thing about today was _____
_____
_____
_____
_____

The funniest thing that happened today was _____
_____
_____
_____
_____

I was really frustrated by _____
_____
_____
_____
_____

71

Are You Talking to Me?

I wish I would have _____

_____

_____

_____

_____

God, I could tell that You were with me today because _____

_____

_____

_____

_____

_____

I'm ready to hear You speak, Lord. What I hear You say through it all is

_____

_____

_____

_____

_____

God, because I heard You, I know that I should _____

_____

_____

_____

_____

A scripture that comes to mind is _____

_____

_____

_____

_____

Day 13
Hip Hip Hooray

When we left for family camp, I never imagined that it would be a painful experience. I'm just glad I took the aspirin along.

It all began with your normal camp things—songs, skits, someone short-sheeting your bed. Then the ropes course opened. It was one of those places that pushes your endurance, challenges you to take risks, and generally requires high liability insurance. The kids were invited to give it a try—with parental supervision, of course.

Five minutes later we were strapping into leg and waist harnesses, while a boy with pimples assured us, "It's perfectly safe. I've been doing this a long time." Long is a relative term when you are nineteen. To him the twentieth century was a long time ago. I was not feeling confident.

"It's very important that your harness is secure. You don't want us to drop you," he cautioned.

"Let's do what he says, Honey," I told my seven-year-old daughter. "After all, he has been doing this a long time."

My oldest son was barely strapped in before he was climbing a tree to the first tightrope, while Hannah and I rechecked the fasteners. With that done she headed straight for The Wall. It was over thirty feet tall, with only one way to the top. You had to hoist yourself up by clinging to small rocks protruding from the side. It was painfully obvious that someone would have to go first to demonstrate for her.

Where was her father? Oh yeah, he was in the horseshoes contest.

As I was being hooked to a safety line, a skinny teenager anchoring the other end assured me that if I fell, she would catch me. I wasn't really buying that. My only hope was that she might slow my descent enough to cushion the impact. I mentally noted that my life insurance was paid up, then reached for the first rock and then the next.

Ten feet into the climb, my anxieties began to lessen. Maybe we wouldn't be collecting after all. Before I knew it, I was halfway up, relaxed and smiling at the crowd that had gathered below me.

I reached for the next rock to keep up my impressive progress, but something was wrong. I could not get hold of it. I stretched and balanced on tiptoe, but I was simply not tall enough to get to the next protrusion. After a few exhausting tries, I contemplated my options. I could climb down in defeat, hang there and hope no one noticed, or jump for it.

Plastered to the wall, out of breath, twenty feet in the air, I was warming to the idea of defeat. Just then, sounds broke through my mental stalemate.

"You can do it, Mom."

"Come on, Kim. Try one more time."

"You're almost there. Keep going."

My friends and my daughter were cheering me onward. Of course, what did they have to lose? Still, I clung to the wall, listening to their encouragement until I started to believe I could do it. With all the strength I had left, I pulled up with one arm and pushed off with my feet, hoping to get enough lift to reach the next stone. In a split second I was airborne, as my foot slipped off the rock. True to her word, the skinny girl did keep me aloft until I splattered against the wall.

Once I got my footing again, the cheering section started back up. My friends kept encouraging, so I kept trying. The cheer that went up as I finally grasped that elusive stone was second only to the cheer I received for reaching the top. At that moment I almost didn't notice my quivering muscles and sore shoulder. I was Super Mom, able to leap tall buildings in a single bound.

As I look back, I realize that I would not have kept going if I had been there alone. The task was too overwhelming, too difficult, and too painful. I succeeded only because I had cheerleaders encouraging me not to give up. Even though they couldn't do it for me, the strength I drew from them made a difference.

Life, too, is full of difficult and overwhelming circumstances that God never intended for us to scale alone. How thankful I am for friends who understand what it means to "encourage the timid" (1 Thes 5:14). The power of a hug, the confidence of a cheer, the courage drawn from a word spoken at the right moment can make the difference between despair and determination. Our climbs may still be exhausting and even painful, yet with cheerleaders they won't be overwhelming.

So grab your pom-poms and cheer someone on today. Or if you're stuck on a wall somewhere, call a friend. The strength to keep going is only a cheer away.

Dear Lord,
Give me eyes to see the people around me I could help with encouraging words. Help me to be a cheerleader to family and friends and even those in my church leadership. Also give me the courage to seek out encouragement when I feel like giving up.

How was God your cheerleader today?
Get a pencil and write it down.

Are You Talking to Me?

~~~~~~~~

Logging the Miles   Today is _____

One word to describe my day would be _____

The greatest thing about today was _____

_____

_____

_____

_____

_____

The funniest thing that happened today was _____

_____

_____

_____

_____

_____

I was really frustrated by _____

_____

_____

_____

_____

_____

I wish I would have _____

_____

_____

_____

_____

Are You Talking to Me?
~~~~~~~~~~

God, I could tell that You were with me today because _____

_____

_____

_____

_____

_____

_____

I'm ready to hear You speak, Lord. What I hear You say through it all is

_____

_____

_____

_____

_____

God, because I heard You, I know that I should _____

_____

_____

_____

_____

_____

_____

A scripture that comes to mind is _____

_____

_____

_____

_____

_____

Day 14

Dr. Jekyll and Mrs. "Weird"

Everything I need to know I learned in kindergarten—not as a student but as a substitute teacher. My instructors were five-year-olds, and the lessons they taught me about human nature are as old as time.

1. Every human being is born with the gossip gene. Though the gene is disguised as tattling at this young age, the principle is the same. Both are founded on the need to tell someone else's business. "Mrs. Weird (they could not say my name without a "d" on the end), Bobby is out of his chair." "Mrs. Weird, Sally isn't supposed to get a drink without asking." "Mrs. Weird, John is at the block center, and he didn't finish his worksheet."

I naively tried to teach these youngsters about the importance of being a loyal friend. As we talked about being trustworthy and faithful, I was interrupted. "Mrs. Weird, Katy has her colors out while you are trying to talk." Somehow they missed the point.

2. Selfish ambition plagues even the very young. The phrase "I'm telling" was second only to "Me first" on their priority list. Whether it was in lining up to leave the room or turning in homework, the future grown-ups wrangled for the best position. They cut in front of one another, gave persuasive speeches about why their table should go to recess first, and finagled any advantage.

Nowhere was this more evident than when we played a phonics game. The competition to be the best was as fierce as any Olympic event. When one child beat out another, the loser's disappointment went unnoticed as the victor celebrated his moment of glory. Who

78

knew correctly reading the word "bad" could feel so good?

3. The human desire to get even is in full bloom by age five. This I discovered when I pried one child from the headlock of another. In explaining why he was choking his classmate, the little boy said, "He tripped me first and it wasn't very nice." I think the gasping offender got the message.

4. No vice is out of the reach of even the youngest in our human race. In the three days I substituted I saw jealousy, anger, hatred, arrogance, cheating, greed, lying, and envy. And that was before snack time. All the stuff of a great soap opera was played out in pigtails and blue jeans. As the Bible puts it, "The acts of the sinful nature are obvious" (Gal 5:19)—even in the very young. This was a harsh lesson in reality.

Yet that isn't all I learned in kindergarten. I also saw the potential that resides inside every human soul. The same child who pushed also shared. The one who wrestled made me a valentine. The compulsive tattlers were also contagious huggers. And all of them were creative and bright.

More stunning, though, was the zeal they had for hearing the Bible story. They had a genuine eagerness as we talked about God. Yet even that did not compare to the sweetness of hearing their voices talking to God. The gentleness and sincerity of their prayers revealed the potential of young lives yielded to God.

Only through His intervention could a nature so bent on selfishness from the very beginning be made righteous. "For the sinful nature desires what is contrary to the Spirit, and the Spirit what is contrary to the sinful nature. They are in conflict with each other" (Gal 5:17). It is a conflict I know all too well.

Thankfully, for those of us who still see glimpses of kindergarten conduct evident in our lives, there is hope.

Those who belong to Christ Jesus have crucified the sinful nature with its passions and desires. [So] since we live by the Spirit [given to us by Christ], let us keep in step with the Spirit.... The fruit of the Spirit [in our lives] is love, joy, peace, patience, kindness, goodness, faithfulness, gentleness and self-control.

GALATIANS 5:24-25, 22-23

Through yielding to that Spirit, the temptation to gossip can be replaced by a self-controlled tongue. Complaints can be overcome by joy; selfish ambition by sacrificial love; and anger by patience and gentleness. Though we may not have practiced these things in kindergarten, or even last week, it's not too late to learn them now.

Dear Lord,
I confess that there are times when I let the sinful part of my nature control my words and actions. Forgive me for letting my selfish desires stand in the way of living by the Spirit. Help me to give up my earthly passions, which stand in the way of producing love, joy, peace, patience, kindness, goodness, faithfulness, gentleness, and self-control in my life. Show me the things I need to let go of.

What did God show you today?
You'd better write that down.

Are You Talking to Me?
~~~~~~~

Logging the Miles   Today is _____

One word to describe my day would be _____

The greatest thing about today was _____

_____

_____

_____

_____

_____

The funniest thing that happened today was _____

_____

_____

_____

_____

_____

I was really frustrated by _____

_____

_____

_____

_____

_____

I wish I would have _____

_____

_____

_____

_____

Are You Talking to Me?
~~~~~~~

God, I could tell that You were with me today because _____

_____

_____

_____

_____

_____

_____

I'm ready to hear You speak, Lord. What I hear You say through it all is

_____

_____

_____

_____

_____

_____

_____

God, because I heard You, I know that I should _____

_____

_____

_____

_____

_____

A scripture that comes to mind is _____

_____

_____

_____

_____

_____

Day 15

Follow the Leader

$\mathcal{A}$ pleasant afternoon at the park took a drastic turn when the kids took the lead.

When we arrived, Hannah and her friend ran to the playground while I finished my lunch in the car. As they frolicked on the monkey bars, I enjoyed the solitude. For fifteen minutes I digested in peace. Then their faces were plastered to the car window, beckoning, "Come on, Mom. We're ready to walk to the creek."

Did I mention how comfortable I was in my bucket seat, listening to the CD, sipping my soda? "You and Christopher haven't even ridden the swings yet. Wouldn't you rather stay at the playground?" I suggested.

I was about to hit the automatic lock when they both gave me *the look*. You know the one I mean. It translates, "Life will be meaningless unless we go to the creek today." Unwilling to be the cause of two wasted lives, I reluctantly gave up my comfortable bucket seat and followed Lewis and Clark down the trail.

Along the way we gathered pecans, felt the breeze, and listened to the birds. It wasn't so bad after all. It was actually kind of nice. When we neared the creek, though, nice got edged out. The kids insisted we take the shortcut through the ditch and over the log, where we could get a better look at the drainage runoff. Truly, the green slime could be seen more clearly from that vantage point.

Finally we reached the peak overlooking the creek, just as the kids drained my soda cup dry. "Can we climb down to the bank to skip rocks?" Christopher asked.

"Sweetie, it's pretty muddy. Your mom will shoot me if you ruin your shoes," I said, hoping we would move along, high and dry.

"We won't get in the mud, really," my daughter added. "Please?" I was being double-teamed.

"OK, but don't get muddy." I stayed on the peak as they picked their way down the hill to the water. There Christopher instructed Hannah on the fine art of rock skipping, but that didn't hold their interest long. They had bigger fish to fry—well, actually, tadpoles.

"Look, Hannah, tadpoles. Miss Kim, can we go to the other side of the creek and see those tadpoles? We won't get our shoes wet," he assured me. "We can cross the water on those rocks."

Ready to nix that idea, I was stopped by *the look*. "If we don't get to hunt tadpoles today, life will be meaningless."

"Be careful, and stay on the rocks. And if your mother gets mad at me, I'm blaming you, Chris." I thought a little guilt might increase his balance. Fortunately, the children proved to be proficient rock jumpers. I watched them maneuver the creek from the rise above until they encountered an obstacle. The stones in the creek were too far apart, and Hannah was stuck in the middle. I was forced to intervene.

I abandoned my perch and climbed down the hill to take her to the other side. I meant only to rescue her, but at their urging I was soon rock jumping with them in pursuit of tadpoles. My concentration was broken when I heard the distinctive sound of a shoe being sucked out of a mud hole.

"You know," Christopher said, as he extricated his foot from the black goo, "if we take off our shoes, they won't get muddy."

How do you argue with that? "And since our shoes would be off," Hannah added, "we could just follow the tadpoles through the water."

Within minutes they were not only out of their shoes but also their jeans. Clad in only tee shirts, they were wading and splashing their way after their quarry. And I was right behind them, my favorite sandals submerged in muddy water, scooping tadpoles into my empty cup. Within minutes I was as wet and dirty as they were.

The nice time at the park I had envisioned was turned upside down by an unforgettable adventure. I was glad I had followed them for a change, instead of them following me. Imagine all the fun I would have missed. And for my trouble I got a hug from my daughter and some words of praise: "You're the best, Mom!"

It makes me wonder about the many roads in life that I've not taken, opting for the predictable over the adventure of following God's lead. The truth is, life is usually less messy when we watch from the bank rather than wading in when God calls. Yet God knew it would take His encouragement to get us out of our comfortable places. So Jesus' command to follow was accompanied by a promise.

"Whoever serves me must follow me [even into murky waters]; and where I am, my servant also will be. *My Father will honor the one who serves me*" (Jn 12:26 emphasis added). Yet he warned bank sitters, "Anyone who does not take his cross and follow me is not worthy of me" (Mt 10:38).

To the one who does follow comes the unspeakable privilege of being honored by God Himself. Yet that honor and the adventure go only to the ones willing to allow God to lead them out of nice and into unknown waters.

Dear Lord,
Help me to be willing to move out of my comfort zone in order to follow You. I know that there is no greater adventure than a life of serving You, wherever You lead. Lead me today so that where You are, I can also be.

Are You Talking to Me?
~~~~~~~

Where did God lead you today?
Don't forget to write about it.

Logging the Miles   Today is _____

One word to describe my day would be _____

The greatest thing about today was _____
_____
_____
_____
_____
_____
_____

The funniest thing that happened today was _____
_____
_____
_____
_____
_____
_____

I was really frustrated by _____
_____
_____
_____
_____
_____
_____

Are You Talking to Me?

I wish I would have _____

_____

_____

_____

_____

God, I could tell that You were with me today because _____

_____

_____

_____

_____

I'm ready to hear You speak, Lord. What I hear You say through it all is

_____

_____

_____

_____

_____

God, because I heard You, I know that I should _____

_____

_____

_____

_____

A scripture that comes to mind is _____

_____

_____

_____

_____

Day 16
Growing Pains

When I awoke one morning, my child was missing. He had been there the night before when I'd turned out his light, tucked him in bed with a kiss, and reminded him to say his prayers. I never dreamed I'd wake to find my little son gone. Yet he was gone, and in his place I found something shocking: a sleeping teenager.

At first I wanted to report that my little boy had been stolen. Realizing that I would need to give his description, I quickly made a mental sketch. I would report that Chase had blonde hair and blue eyes. His cheeks were very chubby, just like his little fingers. It seemed as if it was just yesterday that he fell, learning to ride his bike, so I'm sure he had a scraped knee. He had a contagious giggle and ...

"Mom, what's for breakfast?"

The teenager under the sheets stirred and asked me again, "Mom, what are you going to make for my birthday breakfast?"

No, it couldn't be—and yet those blue eyes did look familiar. The cheeks were no longer chubby, but the hair was just as blonde. It couldn't be! The teenager in the bed was my son, and on his thirteenth birthday he was no longer my little boy.

What an ache I felt in my heart as I stood remembering all the early mornings he had come running into my room to snuggle under the covers with me. Now I was lucky if he made it out of bed in time for lunch. And where were the chubby little hands that used to curl in mine? Suddenly 3'5" had become 5'3".

Yet it wasn't just his size that had changed. Chase was growing up in every way. He used to ask me all the questions on his mind. One of my favorites was, "If God came down and it was raining, would He wear a raincoat?"

He was sure I had the answer. Now that he is older, he's sure that I don't. Interestingly, all of his thirteen-year-old friends are suddenly geniuses. While I know nothing about girls, peer pressure, friends, or anything else that I, of course, have never experienced, they are quoted regularly.

I guess it is all part of growing up. So is his newfound interest in having a presentable room; his fastidiousness about his hair; his ease in conversing with adults; his improved depth of reading material; and most recently his concern over his fashion statement. Yet even in the joy of watching him grow I am tempted to long for the past.

On his birthday, as I sat remembering all of his firsts (first steps, first words, the first time he got lost at Wal-Mart), Chase caught me in my melancholy moment.

"Mom, why are your eyes red?"

"I was just thinking about how fast you're growing up," I said, blinking back a tear. "I'm going to miss you when you're gone."

"Mom," he said with an indulgent tone, "I'm not dead. I'm just thirteen." OK, so he had a point. "Besides," he added, "that's six years away."

There was no use explaining how quickly the years pass to someone who thought it took an eternity for a Pop-Tart to toast. He would eventually learn that lesson, as he had already learned so many others that were turning the little child I adored into an honorable young man I admired.

I guess you could say we're going through growing pains together. We are both learning that while remembering is good, looking to the future is more profitable. It is the only way to grow up to reach all of the potential that the future promises.

Christians, too, are told not to dwell on the past but to "press on to take hold of that for which Christ Jesus took hold of (us), ... forgetting what is behind and straining toward what is ahead" (Phil 3:12-13).

For those who desire the upward call of God, growing up is a lifelong process, one we pursue together.

> The body of Christ [is to] be built up until we all reach unity in faith and in the knowledge of the Son of God and become mature, attaining to the whole measure of the fullness of Christ. Then we will no longer be infants, tossed back and forth by the waves, and blown here and there by every wind of teaching and ... deceitful scheming. Instead, ... we will in all things grow up into Him who is the Head, that is, Christ.
>
> EPHESIANS 4:12-15

God intended that we should never stop growing up, until the day we awake in His presence to find the fullness of His nature in place of our own.

Lord,
Thank You for all the ways You have caused me to grow in my faith, even when some of those ways were painful and scary. Help me not to be satisfied with where I am, but give me a desire to become more fully mature so that in all areas I can stand firm in the truth.

Are You Talking to Me?
~~~~~~~~

How did God help you grow today?
Take out a pencil and write it down.

Logging the Miles   Today is _____

One word to describe my day would be _____

The greatest thing about today was _____

_____

_____

_____

_____

The funniest thing that happened today was _____

_____

_____

_____

_____

I was really frustrated by _____

_____

_____

_____

_____

I wish I would have _____

_____

_____

_____

_____

Are You Talking to Me?
~~~~~~~

God, I could tell that You were with me today because _____

_____

_____

_____

_____

_____

_____

I'm ready to hear You speak, Lord. What I hear You say through it all is

_____

_____

_____

_____

_____

_____

God, because I heard You, I know that I should _____

_____

_____

_____

_____

_____

A scripture that comes to mind is _____

_____

_____

_____

_____

_____

DAY 17
Getting Rooked

When Mayward and Ludie Hembree read the Bible, they took it seriously; and when God gave a command, they knew it was for them. So when these two newlyweds settled on their Oklahoma farm in 1912, they got busy complying with the first command in Genesis: "Be fruitful and increase in number."

Hence, Mayward and Ludie begat Christabel—and Harry, and LaVera, and Winifred, and Warren, and Betty, and Bob, and Harold, and Eddie. From these nine Hembree sons and daughters came twenty grandchildren and a multitude of great-grandchildren, of which I am proud to be one.

Yet a name is not the only thing that Mayward and Ludie passed down. There are other, very distinctive characteristics of a Hembree. First and foremost is the Rook gene. It is the latent tendency to get up a foursome at any hour of the day or night to play Rook and say things like, "Anybody can make 135 points," and, "Are you going to play cards or talk about it?" All true Hembrees have the gene, whether they know it or not.

Case in point: At one family reunion my cousin Becky attended for the first time in twenty-two years. As expected, we reminisced and caught up on the family news. Eventually, however, the pleasantries ended and the Rook game began. Shockingly, Becky had never learned to play Rook. It was a family scandal! A Hembree who had never played Rook?

Why, we Hembrees brag about our Rook prowess. We boast about our skillful trump playing. We crow as we take all 200 points.

Could she be adopted? We would see. Several of us stayed up late one night to teach her the basics.

"OK, Becky. The one takes the fourteen, and the fourteen takes the rook. If your partner has the first two, and you have the Rook, throw him the points, so he can count trumps." She seemed confused. "Remember, if reds are trumps, they take every other color. Even a trump two can take a nontrump fourteen, unless someone trumps that."

The instructions continued until midnight, then we cut her loose and let her solo. Tentatively, she threw out her first trump. It was the Rook to my one! By George, I think she's got it. We finished a whole game, and she never made a careless play. She was a credit to her ancestors. We officially revoked the petition being circulated to remove her from the family.

The next day we held an organized Rook tournament. The idea of having bragging rights until the next reunion appealed to the whole clan. About thirty-five showed up, including Becky. (That's one of the other Hembree traits: fearlessness.)

For two and a half hours the room was filled with tense card play—so tense, in fact, that I gave up my seat to a latecomer and headed for the lake. But not Becky. She moved from table to table, partner to partner, as if she had been born for that very day. And in the end, when the dust settled, it was Becky who reigned supreme.

What a poignant moment as her own father, the toughest Rook player of them all, crowned his own progeny "Rook Queen of the Hembree Clan." She proved to be a real Hembree after all.

I'm pleased to say that my own children have inherited the Rook gene as well. Both my oldest son and my daughter are proficient players. Hannah, who at eight placed fifteenth in the tournament, aspires to wear the Rook crown, "just like cousin Becky."

Sadly, my middle child inherited a less virulent strain of the gene. I blame my husband's family, who play the less intellectual game of poker. Yet all is not lost. Cousin Gary's daughter has a master's in psychology. In time, I believe he can be helped. After all, a Hembree by any other name (like Wier) is still a Hembree. He still has time to imitate his forefathers and prove the family resemblance.

That's exactly what God expects of His own sons and daughters: "Therefore, be imitators of God, as beloved children; and walk in love, just as Christ also loved you and gave Himself up for us" (Eph 5:1, NASB).

Yet how is that possible? How can we be like the invisible God? What would He do with his anger? How would He handle pressure? What would He do about family misunderstandings? How would He react when wronged? Who could really know what God would do?

Jesus said, "The Son can do nothing of Himself, unless it is something He sees the Father doing; for whatever the Father does, these things the Son also does in like manner" (Jn 5:19, NASB).

God the Son is an imitator of God the Father. "He is the image of the invisible God" (Col 1:15, NASB). Jesus proclaimed, "He who has seen me, has seen the Father" (Jn 14:9, NASB).

We can imitate God by imitating Christ. We know how He walked. Scripture tells us. We know how He handled pressure and persecution. His life, His emotions, and His thoughts have all been recorded for us.

The question, then, isn't whether we can resemble the unseen God, but whether we will. If the answer is yes, the family resemblance will be clear.

Father,

You have not only made me part of Your family but You have made me in Your own image. Help me to imitate You by imitating Your Son. Use Your word and Your Holy Spirit to create in me a heart that responds in a way that reflects You to a searching world.

What did God create in you today?
Take out a pencil and record it.

Logging the Miles   Today is _____

One word to describe my day would be _____

The greatest thing about today was _____
_____
_____
_____
_____

The funniest thing that happened today was _____
_____
_____
_____
_____

I was really frustrated by _____
_____
_____
_____
_____

Are You Talking to Me?
~~~~~~~~

I wish I would have _____

_____

_____

_____

_____

God, I could tell that You were with me today because _____

_____

_____

_____

_____

_____

I'm ready to hear You speak, Lord. What I hear You say through it all is

_____

_____

_____

_____

_____

God, because I heard You, I know that I should _____

_____

_____

_____

_____

A scripture that comes to mind is _____

_____

_____

_____

_____

Day 18
Kiss and Tell

A storm was brewing, and it wasn't in the sky. It was in the backseat of my car. I knew it was on the horizon, but still hoped it would go the other way.

It started when I picked my eight-year-old son up after school. "Mom, some kids were teasing me today." I had expected this, sooner or later. What was it, I wondered—his red hair or his freckled complexion, or maybe his skinny physique?

"Oh, Honey, I'm sorry. What were they teasing you about?" I questioned gently, hoping the other kids in the car would be sensitive.

"They were teasing me because I kissed a girl on the lips today," he blustered proudly.

"You did what? Why were you kissing a girl?" I asked, my voice several octaves higher than normal. (The winds were definitely changing.)

"Me and Sarah were blowing in each other's faces, and when we turned at the same time, our lips touched," he giggled. I was about to relax when I heard him whisper to his cousin, "And it felt really good, too."

"I heard that," I said, and the whole car broke into laughter. What was I going to do with this child? Unlike his older brother, he has always noticed the human form. Whether it's a lingerie display at the department store or a swimsuit ad in a catalogue, he usually comments on the brevity of clothes.

Walking through a mall not long ago, he stopped at a video

machine with a buxom babe plastered on the front. "Why does she dress like that, Mom? She has hardly anything on." That was the day I poured out a lesson on modesty.

A few days later he confessed that he had seen some other "immodest" things at the video store. "Do you want me to tell you what I saw?" he asked sheepishly. What he described was beyond immodest. "I'm not going in that aisle anymore, that's for sure," he decided.

Yet all those things were passive experiences. What was I to do about an eight-year-old who liked the way kisses felt? I'd lay down the law, of course. "You know, kisses do feel nice. But at your age, God intends for boys and girls to be just friends. Kissing is something for much later. You will be at least sixteen (or twenty-six) before you're permitted to kiss a girl."

At that my outraged daughter, all of seven, thundered, "Sixteen! I bet you kissed before you were sixteen!" I had almost forgotten that she and a little boy from church had already decided that they were in love and planned to marry. When his mom informed them that they could be only friends for now, they agreed they wouldn't talk about it, but they were definitely getting hitched. I was raining on her parade.

My oldest son, eleven at the time, seemed the least interested. He couldn't imagine why anyone would want to kiss a girl, unless it could get him to the next level on Nintendo, that is. Yet I wasn't fooled. Somewhere in that preadolescent boy lurked the hormones of a teenager, worse than any video villain ever created.

I left my carpool of giggling boys and girls with this thought: "God created many things that are good and right. Love and affection are good things God created, but only at the right time. When you use the right thing at the wrong time, then it becomes *the wrong thing*. Do you understand?"

"Sure, Mom," my little smoocher said, "but it really did feel good."

To be honest, I know what he means. Too often I've had the same experience, enjoying the right thing at the wrong time. For instance, I love spending the day with a good book, even while a project deadline looms. I've been known to eat at my favorite restaurant while the water bill sat unpaid on my desk. I've said yes to too many worthy causes while my kids stayed home with a baby-sitter. Sometimes my own judgment gets clouded.

A little discernment could go a long way in such instances. That is probably why Paul desired it for his flock.

> And this is my prayer: that your love may abound more and more in knowledge and *depth of insight*, so that you may be able *to discern what is best* and may be pure and blameless until the day of Christ.
>
> PHILIPPIANS 1:9-10, *emphasis added*

Like my children, I've learned that just because something is good doesn't mean it is best.

I wish we had to learn that lesson only once. Yet those storm clouds remain on my children's horizons and mine. All we can do is pray for discernment—and keep our umbrellas handy.

Dear Lord,

My life is full of so many blessings. Sometimes I forget that I need to make choices. Give me the discernment to choose not just a good thing but the best thing. Help me not to get distracted by what's pleasing to me. Instead, give me the wisdom to choose what is pleasing to You.

Are You Talking to Me?
~~~~~~~

What wisdom did God give you today?
It's worth writing about.

Logging the Miles   Today is

One word to describe my day would be _____

The greatest thing about today was _____
_____
_____
_____
_____
_____
_____

The funniest thing that happened today was _____
_____
_____
_____
_____
_____
_____

I was really frustrated by _____
_____
_____
_____
_____
_____

Are You Talking to Me?
∽∽∽∽∽∽∽

I wish I would have _____

_____

_____

_____

_____

God, I could tell that You were with me today because _____

_____

_____

_____

_____

_____

I'm ready to hear You speak, Lord. What I hear You say through it all is

_____

_____

_____

_____

_____

God, because I heard You, I know that I should _____

_____

_____

_____

_____

A scripture that comes to mind is _____

_____

_____

_____

Day 19
Ready, Aim, Fire

If you catch a glimpse of Santa flying through the sky, you may not recognize him. I have it on good authority that he has traded in his red suit for black, the traditional color of mourning. You see, there has been a loss at the North Pole. Rudolf has died.

In the frozen wonderland they are calling it homicide, but in East Texas we know what really happened: a hunting accident. Rudolf, apparently here to enjoy our mild weather, was "accidentally" shot while wandering on someone's deer lease. I know this to be true because I have seen the proof. Rudolf, complete with red nose, is hanging over the fireplace in our friend's home. It's shocking, I know, but nonetheless true.

Though this disturbing display doesn't seem to bother our friend's little girls, I can only imagine the horror of their school-mates who come to play. "I have a baby doll, roller skates, the latest action figure, and—oh yeah—Rudolf's head over the fireplace." Eeeeeek!

Not knowing how this news was going to affect the year's sleigh ride (after all, Rudolf was the lead guy), I decided I'd better do my own shopping. For the first time I joined the crowds for the day-after-Thanksgiving shopping—actually, the dawn after Thanksgiving. What I experienced was as shocking as the Rudolf scandal.

It started when I picked my sister up at 5 A.M. You seasoned holiday shoppers already know that special sale items get snatched up in the first fifteen minutes a store is open. And to keep us from loafing on our one day off, the stores open at 6 A.M.

The drive to a nearby town took us half an hour, leaving us plenty of time to bargain hunt, or so I thought. When we arrived, two hundred people were lined up ahead of us at the toy store. We joined them and huddled together in the cold. The crowd seemed pleasant at first, but when an occasional latecomer slid into line with a friend, unrest could be heard. "Can you believe the nerve?" "They need line monitors out here." "She better not get the last Deluxe Magna Doodle!" Magna Doodle? We used to have a Magna Doodle.

Finally the line began to move. All remained orderly until customers reached the front door. Then began a mad dash toward the various aisles. Pushing and shoving were not uncommon, nor was the phrase "I was here first," none of which came from children.

I was able to get the item I wanted, with seemingly no competition, as well as some icicle lights for the house. As I headed toward the counter, however, I heard someone say, "Hurry, I think he is bringing out more Magna Doodles." Suddenly I was overcome with the need for a Deluxe Magna Doodle. They must be wonderful, I thought, everyone here wants one. I hurried behind the crowd and arrived as a clerk was taking down the last carton of six.

A quick count on the aisle told me I would not get a Magna Doodle. However, I was happy to see that a man I recognized from the line outside would get his. His wife had mentioned earlier, "My kids really want that for Christmas."

As I was leaving the store, desperately disappointed at not getting the toy I hadn't even wanted, the man and his wife signaled me. "We were able to get four of them, but we don't really need them all. Would you like one?" WOW! A Deluxe Magna Doodle, on sale!

"I would love to have your extra one," I gushed. I practically floated to the checkout and then to the car. I came back to earth only when my sister asked, "So, who did you buy the Magna Doodle for?"

Who did I buy it for? Was that what she asked? "Well, it's too young for your kids, or mine. And I already have something for the younger cousins."

"Then why did you buy it?" she wondered. Suddenly God revealed my motives, as obvious as Rudolf hanging over the fireplace. "I bought it because ... well, because ... everyone else wanted one. I just felt compelled to get it before they did."

In that moment the unselfish self-portrait that hung in my mind had as many holes in it as my friend's deer. As I felt the sting of God's rebuke, I mourned my image's demise. Fortunately, mistakes are not usually as important as what can be learned from them.

He who listens to a life-giving rebuke will be at home among the wise.... Whoever heeds correction gains understanding.

PROVERBS 15:31-32

What I gained that day was a clear understanding that my selfish nature is lurking just beneath the surface of my unselfish image. If I don't want others to catch a glimpse of it, I better take aim now.

Dear Lord,
Forgive me for the times when I want more than I really need. Help me to be thankful for the abundance You have already given me, and grow in me contentment in my circumstances. Help me to focus on being a giver rather than a getter.

What did God have to say when you focused on Him today? Write about it.

Are You Talking to Me?

Logging the Miles   Today is _____

One word to describe my day would be _____

The greatest thing about today was _____
_____
_____
_____
_____
_____

The funniest thing that happened today was _____
_____
_____
_____
_____
_____

I was really frustrated by _____
_____
_____
_____
_____
_____

I wish I would have _____
_____
_____
_____
_____

Are You Talking to Me?

~~~~~~~~~~

God, I could tell that You were with me today because _____

_____

_____

_____

_____

_____

_____

I'm ready to hear You speak, Lord. What I hear You say through it all is

_____

_____

_____

_____

_____

_____

_____

God, because I heard You, I know that I should _____

_____

_____

_____

_____

_____

A scripture that comes to mind is _____

_____

_____

_____

_____

_____

Day 20
Nitpicker

CAUTION: This story is not for the squeamish. It contains the disturbing account of a vicious assault, not even disclosed to my closest friends. Yet the time has come to share our story, in the hope it will help others. We have been the victims of … lice.

Like me, you may have preconceived ideas about this hair-loving pest. I was in the camp that scorned those who could host such a parasite. "Those who get lice never bathe." "Lice live only in other people's neighborhoods." "Nice people don't talk about lice."

All those myths were shattered when my daughter complained that the itching in her waist-length hair was "making me crazy, Mom." I had noticed her scratching her head but since it was summer, I had assumed it was just dry from all the chlorine in the swimming pool. I finally took a closer look when the itching kept her awake.

When I parted her hair, I was shocked at what I saw. It was a bug party. A big bug party. With big bugs and little bugs, all scrambling for cover. No wonder she couldn't sleep.

She was surprisingly calm. "Can you get them out?" she asked.

"Of course we can," I said, trying to compose myself. "We will just send Daddy to the store to get some special shampoo." While he was gone, I scrambled. "We'll need towels and a brush. I wonder if I should use rubber gloves," I pondered as I scratched my head. Why was I scratching my head? Did it itch, or was it my imagination?

While we waited for her dad, I decided to be honest with my

daughter. "Sweetie, the little bugs in your hair are called lice. It's no big deal, but let's just keep it to ourselves. Let's not tell our friends." I didn't tell her what they might think.

My husband came back with a serious-looking shampoo box and an extra little comb sporting a magnifying glass. "A lady recommended this comb for removing the dead ones and picking out the nits," he said.

"You told someone?" I was aghast. "Does she know you?"

"I've never seen the woman before tonight," he said. Relieved, I got to work. First came the shampoo, then the painstaking task of picking through her hair. What seemed like small brown specks to the naked eye became large, vicious creatures under the lens of the magnifier. It became my mission to uncover, magnify, and purge every beast from her scalp. That done, we disinfected her bedding, combs, brushes, towels, clothes, and hair accessories. All of this would have to be done again, in ten days' time.

During the interval we didn't breath a word of our disgrace. We were careful not to share brushes or spend the night with friends. I even asked my daughter not to scratch in public. Every time my own head itched, I maniacally clawed at it and ran to the mirror, but I never found an uninvited guest. On day ten my phobia got the better of me, and I treated my hair, along with my daughter's.

Though I am happy to report that we are bug free, I am still plagued by the question of how this could happen to us. Did we get it from the swimming pool or someone's hairbrush? Did it come from the ballpark or the amusement park? Could this be a form of biological warfare or some vast right-wing conspiracy? Too embarrassed to talk about it, our questions remained unanswered, all because we—OK, I—feared the scrutiny of others.

How clearly that brings into focus my attitude when a brother or sister in Christ falls prey to something even greater—sin. It is so easy to scorn those who do things we are convinced we would never do. Yet God has some advice to give when uncovering, magnifying, and purging the sin of others.

> Brothers, if someone is caught in a sin, you who are spiritual should restore him *gently*. But watch yourself, or *you also may be tempted*.
>
> GALATIANS 6:1, *emphasis added*

That's good advice for those who have been known to say, "I'd never …"

More often than not, however, our nit-picking isn't a case of the stronger brother restoring the weaker one. It is the pot calling the kettle black. As Jesus more eloquently put it, "Why do you look at the speck of sawdust in your brother's eye and pay no attention to the plank in your own eye?… First take the plank out of your own eye, and then you will see clearly to remove the speck from your brother's eye" (Mt 7:3, 5).

Put the two verses together, and you come up with "walk softly, but don't carry a big stick (in your eye)." In either case, however, the preceding warning holds true. We should approach judging and restoring with CAUTION and leave the magnifying glass at home, lest someone turn it on us.

Dear Lord,
There are times when I am very judgmental. I ignore my own faults, and I focus on the shortcomings of my family and friends. Show me the specks in my own life that You know need to be removed. Give me a gentle spirit when it comes to helping others remove theirs.

Are You Talking to Me?
~~~~~~~

What did God show you today?
It's Worth Writing Down.

Logging the Miles   Today is _____

One word to describe my day would be _____

The greatest thing about today was _____
_____
_____
_____
_____
_____
_____

The funniest thing that happened today was _____
_____
_____
_____
_____
_____
_____

I was really frustrated by _____
_____
_____
_____
_____
_____
_____

Are You Talking to Me?
~~~~~~~

I wish I would have _____

_____

_____

_____

_____

God, I could tell that You were with me today because _____

_____

_____

_____

_____

I'm ready to hear You speak, Lord. What I hear You say through it all is

_____

_____

_____

_____

_____

God, because I heard You, I know that I should _____

_____

_____

_____

_____

A scripture that comes to mind is _____

_____

_____

_____

_____

Day 21
ATM Blues

I recently read that many experts predict America will one day be a totally cashless society. That would mean no more digging in the cup holder for change or pawning off your pennies on the pizza guy. Cash, they believe, will be as obsolete as the eight-track tape.

Many of us have already begun to phase cash out of our lives. We prefer credit cards and debit cards, electronic transfers and bank drafts. And, of course, there is my all-time favorite, the checkbook.

It works any time, day or night. It's easy to use and versatile. No amount is too big or too small for a check, although my husband really hates it when I write a sixty-one cent check for an Icee. Yet that is the beauty of it. It's always with you, just waiting to be used. Chinese take-out? I've got a check. Girl Scout cookies? I've got a check. Cute little open-toed sandals on sale? I've got a check.

Not only do checks offer freedom and convenience, they also are available in a plethora of styles. We have always used those boring green checks that come with the account, but not long ago I decided to break out of that rut.

We needed a style to reflect our family's personality. I chose the Looney Tunes checks. One month later, at my husband's urging, I switched to the Bible Hero series. We're now back to green. They're practical yet drab.

I think my husband hopes my distaste for their appearance will discourage me from writing so many. It hasn't worked. Yet I've thought of something that might, something I saw my grand-parents do—spend cash.

How hard could it be to manage a cash budget? I estimated what we would need for a week's worth of groceries, then added enough for two meals at a restaurant plus an extra twenty-dollar buffer—just in case. Then I withdrew the whole thing at one time.

I was so excited about my new cash budget system when I left the bank. I immediately had to try it. First I stopped by the convenience store and paid cash for an Icee. Then my daughter and I used one of our restaurant allocations.

I had forgotten to plan two dollars to buy crickets for my son's class terrarium, so I had to dip into my buffer sooner than I had planned. Later that day I also remembered that my children needed new Bibles. That set me way back, but if I shopped carefully, I was sure I could stretch what was left over the remaining six days.

On the way home we stopped by the super center to pick up our groceries. That's where my new system hit a snag. I might have been able to get the food with what was left, but then I remembered a few more necessities—dog food, hair spray, laundry soap, stain remover, poster board—and they just happened to have that cassette tape I'd been looking for.

When I checked out, I was thirty dollars short. I had no checkbook, no credit card, and no ATM card. Fortunately, my son's wallet was in my purse.

I left the store and headed back to the bank. I got enough money to repay my son, plus an amount equal to my original withdrawal. Surely that would last me six more days. I'll spare you the details, but by noon on day two I had given up the cash system and retrieved my checkbook. In principle I still believe dealing in cash may be the most financially responsible method of spending, but putting it into practice apparently requires more discipline than I have. I think it's best to leave that approach to people with a little more experience.

That's how I feel sometimes when it comes to spiritual disciplines such as prayer and Bible study. In theory they are great ideas, but putting them into practice can be a challenge. One minute Jesus is walking on water, and the next I'm sound asleep. I start out praying for my family, and before I know it I'm making my to-do list.

While I may be tempted to think that the answer is to leave those spiritual disciplines to people with more experience, Scripture offers a different answer to my dilemma:

> Therefore, let us leave the elementary teaching about Christ and go on to maturity.... We do not want you to become lazy, but to imitate those who through faith and patience inherit what has been promised.

> HEBREWS 6:1, 12

God's answer to those who struggle with spiritual maturity is not for them to leave it to more experienced Christians but to imitate those Christians, through faith, practice, and patience. Maturity takes time, but Christ "sympathize(s) with our weaknesses" and responds by offering us "mercy and ... grace ... in our time of need" (Heb 4:15-16). So "do not throw away your confidence; it will be richly rewarded" (Heb 10:35).

Now that is a future prediction you can count on.

Dear Lord,
Too many times I have neglected the spiritual things that seem so hard for me. I confess that I have been lazy in my faith. Give me the desire and strengthen my will so that I might move out of my baby faith and into a mature faith. Make me someone others can look to when their own faith needs to be strengthened.

Are You Talking to Me?

How did God strengthen you today?
Write about it.

Logging the Miles   Today is _____

One word to describe my day would be _____

The greatest thing about today was _____

_____

_____

_____

_____

_____

_____

The funniest thing that happened today was _____

_____

_____

_____

_____

_____

_____

I was really frustrated by _____

_____

_____

_____

_____

_____

Are You Talking to Me?

I wish I would have _____

_____

_____

_____

_____

God, I could tell that You were with me today because _____

_____

_____

_____

_____

I'm ready to hear You speak, Lord. What I hear You say through it all is

_____

_____

_____

_____

_____

God, because I heard You, I know that I should _____

_____

_____

_____

_____

A scripture that comes to mind is _____

_____

_____

_____

_____

Day 22
Cheese and Whine

There are certain things one should be aware of when considering mountain biking. First, a mountain is involved. Second, mountain bikes don't have training wheels. And third, it's a long way down. Without an understanding of these factors, abrasions and even dismemberment could follow. Our run down Colorado's Purgatory Mountain, now dubbed the Trail of Whimpers, had its harrowing moments.

On our vacation the kids and I found ourselves looking for an alternative activity when my husband and father-in-law went on an all-day scenic train ride. Sitting for hours didn't appeal to my three kids and their cousin. They wanted to do something more interactive, so we decided on mountain biking.

We arrived at the bike shop early and ready for fun, but the folks at the bike shop seemed awfully serious as they outfitted us with protective gear and custom-sized bikes. "Have you ever been mountain biking, Ma'am?" the guide asked.

"No, but sometimes I ride my Schwinn to the mailbox," I replied.

He wasn't amused. Instead he gave us a crash course in the proper operation of mountain bikes. Mine had twenty-seven gears and two braking systems. "Always use the back brake first," he warned. "Otherwise you will flip headfirst over the handlebars."

Suddenly I was all ears. "And be sure to switch to a lower gear when you go uphill."

Whoa there, partner! We had no intentions of riding up the mountain. "We are taking the lift to the top and riding down," I reminded him. His only response was to nod and request my signature on a liability release form. Before I could ponder the significance of statements like "will not hold us responsible for injury or death," the kids were urging me to catch up as they headed toward the lifts. So, with a quick scribble on the dotted line, I joined my children.

When we unloaded at the top of the lift, our bikes, which had been sent ahead of us, were waiting. The kids adjusted their helmets and set their gears for the downhill ride, and I consulted the trail map. The guide had told us to stay on Brush Rake Loop, the beginner's trail. I located the sign and we were off.

It wasn't long before we were convinced we were on the wrong trail. Around every corner was a new incline. I didn't understand how we could be on the right path if we had to pedal upward so often. I had pictured effortlessly coasting down the hill. It was much harder than we had expected. That's when the whining began. "It's hot. This is hard. I'm hungry. How much longer?" Then the kids started whining, too.

Needing a break, we stopped to eat the cheese sandwiches in my backpack. After our lunch we decided we needed a break from the bikes, so we went on a hike instead. We had a wonderful adventure, discovering creeks, conquering hills, and collecting wildflowers. Eventually, though, we knew we had to get back on the bikes for our ride up the downhill. As we were starting off again, we noticed two signs down the path. One affirmed that we were indeed on Brush Rake Loop. The other said, "Forest Service Road, Easiest Way to the Base." After a unanimous vote we were on the wide gravel road and finally riding downhill.

Now the problem was controlling our speed on the steep grades.

The kids were a little shaky at first, but after a while they became comfortable with their hand brakes. Hannah, who was only seven, was the only one struggling to manage her bike. As long as she moved at a snail's pace she felt secure, so I stayed back with her while the boys went a little ways ahead.

When my daughter and I rounded the next curve, we couldn't see the boys. The only thing on the path was a service truck, which had stopped and was backing up. I watched as two men jumped out and ran to the edge of the road. My heart stopped as I realized someone must have gone over the edge. Was it the boys? Around the last curve the drop-off had been at least a hundred feet. From where I was in the middle of the road, I couldn't tell if we were still on the edge of that cliff.

I sped up just as the men pulled Bailey and his bike out of the gully into which he had driven. Mercifully, it had been only a five-foot drop into a grove of ferns, but nonetheless it was scary for an eight-year-old careening out of control.

With tears and a few scrapes he explained what had happened. "I just wanted to go a little faster and then I couldn't stop. My bike went out of control and I fell off the road," he said, crying harder. "I just want to ride with you and Hannah."

As we got back on the bikes, the other two boys, who had doubled back to see what was taking so long, arrived. We decided that we would stick together the rest of the way down so that no one else lost control.

Life is so often like that winding mountain road; full of unexpected turns and dangerous drop-offs. Navigating through it can be a hazardous journey, especially when we lose control.

There are so many crashes I could have avoided in my life if I had just put on the brakes at the right time. Like Bailey, though, I had to learn that lesson the hard way. How much better it would have been to have just paid attention to the instructions I was given.

> Knowing God leads to self-control. Self-control leads to patient endurance, and patient endurance leads to godliness.... So, dear brothers and sisters, work hard to prove that you really are among those God has called and chosen. Doing this, you will never stumble or fall away.
>
> 2 PETER 1:6, 10, NLT

Without an understanding of these factors, whining, heartbreak, and even emotional scars are sure to follow.

Lord,
You know the places in my life where I am not practicing self-control.
Help me to give those areas over to You so that I can avoid hurts to myself
and to others. Let me be known as someone who is self-controlled in
speech and deed.

What did you turn over to God today?
Turn the page and write about it..

Are You Talking to Me?

~~~~~~

Logging the Miles   Today is _____

One word to describe my day would be _____

The greatest thing about today was _____

_____

_____

_____

_____

_____

The funniest thing that happened today was _____

_____

_____

_____

_____

_____

I was really frustrated by _____

_____

_____

_____

_____

I wish I would have _____

_____

_____

_____

_____

_____

Are You Talking to Me?
~~~~~~~~

God, I could tell that You were with me today because _____

_____

_____

_____

_____

_____

_____

_____

I'm ready to hear You speak, Lord. What I hear You say through it all is

_____

_____

_____

_____

_____

_____

God, because I heard You, I know that I should _____

_____

_____

_____

_____

A scripture that comes to mind is _____

_____

_____

_____

_____

_____

Day 23
The King

Our family has become known as an easy mark where unwanted, lost, or homeless animals are concerned. We never turn away a creature in need. Because of this reputation, a friend called and asked if we would adopt her pet. It violated her lease and needed a new home. If we didn't take it, she would have to turn it over to the pound. The very idea of a homeless pet brought an immediate response to my lips.

"We'd be glad to."

The next day she arrived to introduce our newest family member, a ferret. We had seen these weasely creatures at the pet store but had never actually held one. So when she handed him to me, I was completely unprepared for the attack. Within seconds I was overtaken, not by his sharp claws or long teeth but by his odor. My olfactory senses were assaulted in the most merciless way.

I quickly put him down and, not wanting to offend, said something like, "He has a very distinct aroma, doesn't he?"

At that she handed me his special ferret shampoo and told me a bath would take care of the smell. Relieved, I turned my attention toward the critter exploring every nook and cranny of the house.

Over the next few days we began observing the habits of our new pet. The first thing we noticed was that when he scampered across the floor, his back hips had a very pronounced swivel. This earned him his new name, Elvis. It was very appropriate, since he also behaved as if he was the king of the house. There wasn't one room he didn't claim as conquered territory, banishing both cats and dogs to exile. Whenever the other pets saw Elvis coming, they hightailed it to the back door, hoping for an escape.

The only exception was our dog Baby. She was quite amused by the antics of the king and regularly joined him. The two would race up and down the stairs and engage in wrestling matches as entertaining as any WWF event. Baby may have had the weight advantage, but Elvis had the brains. He brought that dog to the mat every time with one strategic bite on Baby's upper lip.

When Baby was not around, Elvis found other activities to entertain himself. His favorite game was "sock-it-to-me." With what can only be described as sock radar, Elvis honed in on socks left on the floor. As quick as lightning, he would dart from under furniture, grab the sock, and disappear. As long as there were socks on the floor, and at my house there was an ample supply, his sock reconnaissance mission continued.

One day, Elvis found our sock basket in the laundry room. It was like hitting the mother lode. All afternoon he moved socks to various hiding places around the house. It made him so happy. Unfortunately, when we couldn't find the soccer socks on game day, Elvis' game ceased to be amusing.

There were other drawbacks to our frisky friend. He was nearly impossible to find when he hid. He never came when we called him. To let him roam free meant putting a litter pan in every room, and he had a bad habit of nibbling on my ankles.

By far, though, the worst thing about owning a ferret was the offensive odor. I did my best to get rid of it. I bathed him in the special shampoo and sprayed him with ferret deodorizer, but within twenty-four hours the smell always came back.

A little investigation uncovered the problem. You see, ferrets have musk glands that continually produce a very distinct odor. Elvis and his smell were inseparable. I could cover it up temporarily, but I couldn't get rid of it. Wherever that ferret went, his odor was sure to go. Eventually that is what happened. Fed up with all the baths, Elvis and his odor escaped out the front door one fine spring morning. I am convinced that he found another runaway ferret that thinks he smells just dandy.

Believe it or not, we Christians have an odor, too. Ours, however, is not one we want to get rid of.

> But thanks be to God, who always leads us in triumphal procession in Christ [our King] and through us spreads everywhere the fragrance of the knowledge of him. For we are to God the aroma of Christ among those who are being saved and among those who are perishing.
>
> 2 CORINTHIANS 2:14-15

As we live the truth of the gospel, every day reflecting Christ's image, we send out a fragrant aroma that reveals God to those around us. Yet don't be surprised if a few people hold their noses, because not everyone will find that fragrance pleasant.

> To the one [who rejects Christ] we are the smell of death; to the other, the fragrance of life.... Unlike so many, we do not peddle the word of God for profit. On the contrary, in Christ we speak before God with sincerity, like men sent from God.
>
> 2 CORINTHIANS 2:16-17

Either way we are called to walk triumphantly and speak of our Savior, that the very fragrant yet distinct aroma of Christ will precede us wherever we go.

Are You Talking to Me?
~~~~~~~~

Lord,
Help me be the sweet aroma of Christ's love to those in my world. Give
me confidence and sincerity so that I might speak of Your Son whether I
am welcomed or rejected.

How was God a sweet aroma to you today?
Get a pencil and write it down.

Logging the Miles   Today is _____

One word to describe my day would be _____

The greatest thing about today was _____
_____
_____
_____
_____
_____

The funniest thing that happened today was _____
_____
_____
_____
_____

I was really frustrated by _____
_____
_____
_____
_____

Are You Talking to Me?

~~~~~~~~

I wish I would have _____

_____

_____

_____

_____

God, I could tell that You were with me today because _____

_____

_____

_____

_____

I'm ready to hear You speak, Lord. What I hear You say through it all is

_____

_____

_____

_____

_____

God, because I heard You, I know that I should _____

_____

_____

_____

_____

A scripture that comes to mind is _____

_____

_____

_____

Day 24
That's a Spicy Meatball

There was so much to do, so little time, and even less help. My only hope was that nothing would go wrong.

My husband left town on business, confident that I could manage the big night without him. After all, we were just talking about getting ready for two parties. One of them, though, happened to be our son's first dance. That, in itself, made me apprehensive. Even though a trustworthy Christian family was hosting it, I wasn't convinced that thirteen-year-olds could or should dance. It was with trepidation, and many conditions, that permission was granted.

If getting him ready wasn't enough for one evening, I had also promised to make food for a friend's surprise fortieth birthday party. I had just enough time to deliver the food, come home, change into party clothes, take Chase to his dance, interrogate the mother hosting the dance, and arrive at my friend's party in time to yell "surprise."

I quickly loaded everything in the car—the shrimp, the taquitos, the guacamole, the chocolate cake, and the hot wok full of spicy Italian meatballs. Rushing out the door, I promised Chase I would return in fifteen minutes. Soon I was out of my neighborhood and onto the highway. Just then some brilliant person slammed on his brakes in front of me. I, in turn, slammed on mine. While my car was still screeching to a stop, I looked into the backseat, screaming NOOOOOO, as I helplessly watched every single meatball slosh out of the toppled wok.

I immediately swerved into the median and stopped in the middle of the highway. I couldn't go back to the house, but I couldn't go on without the meatballs. I did not have time for this problem. There was only one thing I could do. I climbed into the backseat and began the salvage effort. In a hurry, I reached both hands into the meatballs to scoop them out of the floorboard and back into the wok. Mama Mia! Was that ever a mistake. In an instant I was out of the car, flinging boiling-hot sauce off my burning hands and onto passing cars.

When the feeling returned to my fingers, I climbed back in the car and cautiously picked up one meatball at a time and placed it back in the wok. About two-thirds of the dish was salvageable, leaving the remainder smeared around the backseat. Using a dirty soccer sock for a towel, I wiped my hands and made the short drive to the party. As I finally unloaded my scrambled cargo, grumbling as I did so, my friends got a laugh out of the sauce on my elbows and in my hair. Very funny. We'll see who has the last laugh when they find out they have eaten meatballs that rolled around the floor of my car.

Worse than the meatball disaster, though, was the realization that I no longer had time to drive Chase to his first dance. An emergency call to his grandmother gave her that honor. Taking a shower and cleaning the car suddenly became a higher priority for me. I didn't even arrive at my own party until after the guest of honor had been surprised and the last meatball had been consumed—not that I was planning to eat one.

Besides, I didn't have much of an appetite. My mind was preoccupied imagining the junior high dance scene. I pictured girls in black leather pants, loud rock and roll, and parents tied up in the closet. I looked at my watch and realized I still had one hour until the dance ended. As anxious as I was to find out what was really going on, I knew I couldn't show up early without totally humiliating my son. So I did what I had been doing all night in the face of my trials. I persevered.

Sometimes staying the course in the small things can build as much character as persisting in the bigger things. Picking up one more dirty towel off the floor. Enduring one more criticism. Teaching someone, one more time, to share. Helping with math facts night after night. Lovingly forgiving one more hurt. Serving at church when you would rather quit. Reading God's Word when understanding is slow.

Such things are all just a training ground for the bigger trials that are sure to come our way. Yet for those who have learned to patiently keep on keeping on, a reward awaits.

Blessed is the [one] who perseveres under trial; for once he has been approved, he will receive the crown of life which the Lord has promised to those who love Him.

JAMES 1:12, NASB

Though I won't tell you about the dance until tomorrow, I can tell you that a few Italian meatballs won't steal the crown from this Mama Mia.

Lord,
Sometimes I feel overwhelmed by all of the daily trials that come my way. I want to persevere, yet sometimes I am discouraged. Help me see the benefits to my character and to Your kingdom that result from my faithful endurance. Make me steadfast, Lord, so that I may receive the blessings You have promised in this life and the one to come.

Are You Talking to Me?
~~~~~~~~

How did God bless you today?

Logging the Miles

Today is _____

One word to describe my day would be _____

The greatest thing about today was _____

_____

_____

_____

_____

_____

The funniest thing that happened today was _____

_____

_____

_____

_____

I was really frustrated by _____

_____

_____

_____

_____

I wish I would have _____

_____

_____

_____

_____

God, I could tell that You were with me today because _____

_____

_____

_____

_____

_____

_____

I'm ready to hear You speak, Lord. What I hear You say through it all is

_____

_____

_____

_____

_____

_____

God, because I heard You, I know that I should _____

_____

_____

_____

_____

_____

_____

A scripture that comes to mind is _____

_____

_____

_____

_____

_____

Day 25

Boogie, Man

"There is a time for every activity under heaven: ... a time to mourn and a time to dance" (Eccl 3:1,4). Solomon said it, but we lived it. As my son prepared to attend his first dance, I mourned that the day had come—and then I started the dance lessons. You can imagine how excited my thirteen-year-old was to be dancing with his mother. Still, his lack of experience necessitated my help.

"When you ask a girl to dance," I said, trying to make eye contact with his dodging glance, "offer her your left hand. Then lightly rest your other hand on her waist."

When I extended my hand and Chase didn't move, I pulled him up from the sofa and correctly positioned his hands, giving him an exhaustive list about where not to put his hands. My son would exhibit good taste in the spirit of Fred Astaire and Ginger Rogers.

At that, the actual dance lesson commenced. Three steps into the demonstration Chase pulled away and dropped onto the couch with his arms folded across his chest. "OK, OK, I got it, Mom," he said with a slightly flushed face. I guess he didn't want my pointers on the Macarena. Oh well, time was short anyway.

When he was finally ready to leave, I gave him some final words of advice.

"Be sure to thank Taylor for inviting you to her birthday dance. Be a good guest. Dance at least once, but keep your distance. Are you sure you want to go?"

"I'm going to be late, Mom. I need to leave now." As he left with his grandmother, I wondered if he would heed any of my advice.

The next three hours crawled by. I had my own party to attend, but all I could think about was the dance. I pictured a dark room, with only enough light to see the scantily dressed girls prowling the unchaperoned hall. I was anxious to see it for myself, but I knew I couldn't arrive early. So I toughed it out until ten o'clock.

When I did arrive, things were, of course, above reproach. This Christian family had provided a very tasteful and wholesome atmosphere. The lights were only moderately dimmed. Parents were as thick as thieves, and the girls' attire was very unshocking. My son, far from rabble-rousing, was slouched in a chair, hands folded across his chest, doing that thing guys do when they want to appear cool.

When he saw me, he gave an aloof nod of recognition that always warms my heart. Before I could get to him, though, a girl approached my son. As she asked him to slow dance, I could feel the hair on the back of my neck bristle. My son stood, but before he could offer her his hand, the girl draped herself around his neck in a very un-Ginger-like posture.

I would have cut in and rescued my son but for one amusing complication. This girl was so close to him that he couldn't put his hands on her waist. Instead, his elbows rested at her waist and he couldn't decide what to do with his hands. Clasp them? Put them on her back? Slide them in his pockets? No. He just let them flail in midair behind her for the duration of the song. That priceless moment was too good to interrupt.

While I waited, one girl after another asked him to dance. Eventually Chase even asked the birthday girl. It was the first time all night he got to be Fred Astaire and hold his hand out first. With that final spin around the floor, my son's foray into dancing ended, at least for the foreseeable future. Experience tells us that arm-in-arm dancing is something best left for much later.

Chase's thoughts about the evening were best summed up in a conversation he had with his dad.

"So, I hear you danced with a girl last night," Tony said.

"Nope," Chase replied. "I danced with five."

At that they exchanged a high five.

I can only imagine what the next few years will bring in the life of my maturing son. Though I am cautious, I am also thankful that I remember what it was like to be a teenager. I can and do sympathize with him. Together, my husband and I hope to guide him with our collective voice of experience.

In our own uncertain times as believers, we, too, can be guided by the voice of the One who has experienced all things.

Since then we have a great high priest who has passed through the heavens, Jesus the Son of God, let us hold fast our confession. For we do not have a high priest who cannot sympathize with our weaknesses, but one who has been tempted in all things, as we are, yet without sin. Let us therefore draw near with confidence to the throne of grace that we may receive mercy and may find grace to help in time of need.

HEBREWS 4:14-16, NASB

He knows what it is to be rejected, persecuted, tempted, alone, threatened, misunderstood, and grief-stricken. There is no test man can face that Christ has not endured and overcome sinlessly.

If life is our dance, Christ alone is qualified to be our Instructor.

Dear Lord,
Thank You that in Your wisdom Christ first experienced every kind of joy and trial I will ever experience. I trust You to guide me through the days to come and to prepare me for the new challenges that face me.

Are You Talking to Me?
~~~~~~~

Where did God guide you today?
Get a pencil and write it down.

Logging the Miles   Today is _____

One word to describe my day would be _____

The greatest thing about today was _____

_____

_____

_____

_____

The funniest thing that happened today was _____

_____

_____

_____

_____

I was really frustrated by _____

_____

_____

_____

_____

I wish I would have _____

_____

_____

_____

_____

Are You Talking to Me?
~~~~~~~~

God, I could tell that You were with me today because _____

_____

_____

_____

_____

_____

_____

I'm ready to hear You speak, Lord. What I hear You say through it all is

_____

_____

_____

_____

_____

_____

God, because I heard You, I know that I should _____

_____

_____

_____

_____

_____

_____

A scripture that comes to mind is _____

_____

_____

_____

_____

_____

Day 26
Campfire Girls

Years ago, when I was newly married with no children, three friends and I went on a girls-only camping trip. Our husbands packed the tent, cook stove, and lantern and gave us a crash course on tent assembly, then we were off, waving good-bye to four snickering spouses.

I failed to see what was amusing. Was it our sense of adventure, our independence, or the curling irons and makeup bags? We didn't ask. We just popped the tops of the sodas and pointed the car toward Davy Crocket National Forest.

We arrived with just enough daylight left to erect the tent. It took three tries to put it together without having any poles left over, but once it was up it was solid. By nightfall we had worked up an appetite and were ready for some camp cuisine—hotdogs and chips and dip. Only one thing was missing—the campfire.

We scoured the area for enough sticks to start a cozy blaze, then we gathered around on lawn chairs for a good old weenie roast. We ate and sang and laughed about how we would gloat when we got home. It was a true bonding experience.

As we congratulated ourselves for being hearty campers, the fire began to dwindle. I took it upon myself to stir the embers, but the fire simply would not flare up. It needed something. Maybe more sticks, or pine straw, or lantern fuel. Against the better judgment of my friends, I grabbed the fuel can and splashed up a few flames. It created the perfect fire. Each time the fire would die down, I was ready with the fuel can.

One anxious friend cautioned me, "You really ought to be careful. You are going to catch yourself on fire." Another echoed, "I really don't think that is a good idea." I joked, "Lighten up. The worst that could happen would be that the flames would run up the fuel stream and explode the can."

The words still hung in the air as that very thing happened. The flames raced up the fuel to the top of the can. In a panic, I threw it to the ground. Flames ignited the pool of spilled fuel, and we all ran for cover. Stunned, we watched the fire spread to a nearby tree. In seconds it was out of our control. After momentary panic, we got in the car and headed for the ranger's booth.

I don't know why no one stayed with the fire. Maybe because we didn't want to be maimed when the fuel can exploded. All reason went out the window as we piled in and drove at breakneck speed over dark, narrow roads and axle-breaking speed bumps. I was in the front seat, chanting over and over, "I can't believe I did that. You all told me not to do that."

I had to think. What should we do? How was I going to fix this? There was nothing I could do. Then I heard one of my friends mumbling in the backseat.

"Will you please stop whimpering?" I snapped. "It's going to be OK."

Then came the quiet reply. "She's praying." Praying? I just burned down a national forest. She's praying? I wish I had thought of that. We all prayed, together begging God to intervene, to protect the forest and other campers. Praying like that was new to me. It seemed right, but truthfully, I wasn't expecting much.

When we got to the check-in station, an elderly ranger was on duty. The car skidded to a stop, and I yelled out the window, "There's a huge fire on Lob Lolly Loop. Call the fire department." He did just that, and we raced back to our campsite. In minutes we could hear the sirens advancing, but we were already back to the fire—or were we?

Where was the fire? That was our tent, our lawn chairs. As we got out of the car, two men approached. "What happened to that huge fire?" I asked, very confused.

"We heard the commotion and saw some flames," they explained. "So we walked over and stomped it out." As it turns out, lantern fuel isn't combustible. It could not have exploded. What spilled had burned off, but most of the fuel stayed in the can. The strangers stomped out the brush that caught fire. The only significant damage was a charred pine tree.

How embarrassing. What were the words I had said to the park ranger? "Huge. It's a huge fire." The sirens were getting closer. The park ranger pulled up. Why were they all looking at me?

"Well, young lady, I hope you've learned a lesson," scolded Mr. Ranger. "I'll have to take your name in case the fire department wants to bill you for the call." Thankfully, he intercepted the hook-and-ladder truck before they could scold me too.

I was impulsive. I was stubborn. I was so embarrassed. Yet even more than that, I was humbled at what God had done for me. I had used poor judgment, and I had ignored the counsel of my friends. I had no right to expect God to intervene. In truth, it didn't even occur to me to ask. Yet He reached into my self-absorbed world to show me His desire to be in the midst of my fiery ordeals, teaching me a much-needed lesson.

The Lord is near. Don't worry about anything, instead, pray about everything. Tell God what you need and thank him for all he has done. If you do this, you will experience God's peace, which is far more wonderful than human minds can understand. His peace will guard your hearts and minds as you live in Christ Jesus.

PHILIPPIANS 4:5-6, LB

How young I was, not only in age but also in my experience with God. Yet how mercifully He showed me His availability when all that was at stake was a forest. Since then the stakes have been bigger, the fires hotter, the potential consequences greater. Yet when they burn out of control, consuming my strength and leaving me helpless, I don't have to despair. "Great is our Lord and abundant in strength; His understanding is infinite" (Ps 147:5, NASB), even if we sometimes light those fires with our own hands.

Father in Heaven,
So many times it has been Your mighty right hand that has upheld me.
Thank You for Your mercy and Your perfect provisions. Thank You that
You are always near and ready to hear my call. I can dwell in peace
because Your strength is abundant and You understand my deepest needs.

How did God uphold you today? Write it down.

Are You Talking to Me?

Logging the Miles   Today is _____

One word to describe my day would be _____

The greatest thing about today was _____

_____

_____

_____

_____

_____

The funniest thing that happened today was _____

_____

_____

_____

_____

_____

I was really frustrated by _____

_____

_____

_____

_____

_____

I wish I would have _____

_____

_____

_____

_____

Are You Talking to Me?
∽∽∽∽∽∽∽

God, I could tell that You were with me today because _____

_____

_____

_____

_____

_____

_____

I'm ready to hear You speak, Lord. What I hear You say through it all is

_____

_____

_____

_____

_____

_____

God, because I heard You, I know that I should _____

_____

_____

_____

_____

_____

_____

A scripture that comes to mind is _____

_____

_____

_____

_____

_____

Day 27
Double Trouble

What sounded like the ideal situation turned out to be more than I bargained for. Our relocating neighbors offered us the use of their pool in exchange for "just keeping it clean" until the house sold.

I jumped at the chance to use their pool all summer and took full responsibility for the deal. "This is going to be a breeze," I told my husband after our friends gave me a ten-minute crash course in pool maintenance. After all, how hard could it be to keep twenty thousand gallons of water sparkling blue?

I found out the very first week, when a little algae appeared in the water. Actually it was a lot of algae that, overnight, had turned the water murky. My response to the problem was to add more chlorine. I also ran the pumps ten hours a day instead of three. It helped a little, but I still couldn't see the bottom of the pool.

More chemicals had to be the answer. At the store there are a variety of toxic remedies. I decided on an all-purpose shock treatment. I used three packages. The next day it definitely looked better, but the water was far from either sparkling or blue. I shocked it one more time, but twenty-four hours later it looked the same. Just as I was fretting over how to solve the problem, a new one arose.

After our neighbors moved away, we were the only ones given permission to use the pool. Imagine our surprise, then, when we noticed a large group of teenage boys frolicking in my science experiment. My husband stepped in and firmly explained to these strangers that the pool was private property and off-limits. They hesitantly got out of our green water, only to return the next day and the next.

This "breeze" of a job was starting to get a little stormy. Why had I said yes again? Oh yeah, sparkling blue water, swim any time, yada, yada, yada. If only I had anticipated all the trouble it would be.

The only thing to do was to invest more time and resources. We put up "no trespassing" signs and patrolled the pool obsessively. Every time I passed the house, I was compelled to stop. Since I had neglected to find out how to set the times on the pump, I had to walk over every morning to turn them on, and I had to go back to turn them off every afternoon. I also invested in more chlorine tablets, though my neighbors had thought theirs would last all summer. Oddly enough, they ran out in two weeks.

I kept up my vigil, all the while becoming increasingly disillusioned with my end of the bargain. The low point came when the water caused two ear infections and an unexplained skin rash. Discouraged, I relayed my frustration to someone else. She, in turn, called a friend who happened to be a licensed pool doctor, or something like that. I frankly think she was a genius. After a ten-minute analysis, she diagnosed the problem.

"You have mustard algae." How awful! "And your chlorine level is about four times what it ought to be." How could that have happened? "All you need is an algaecide, and it will be sparkling blue in twenty-four hours." With that my problem was solved. As promised, the water sparkled again the next day. With my genius only a phone call away, we enjoyed an algae-free pool until the house finally sold at the end of the summer.

For years I approached my Christian life the way I approached the pool commitment. Like most, I was drawn to Jesus Christ because He offers what can't be obtained anywhere else—forgiveness, mercy, and grace. What wonderful free gifts made available at His expense to all who believe! Yet it took a while longer for me to understand that there are two sides to that coin.

I knew that God would "love me with an everlasting love." Yet what a surprise to be told, "Do not marvel if the world hates you." That's not fair! I signed up for the promise. I'm sure I was told, "You will receive treasures in heaven," but no one announced, "Blessed are those who are hungry now."

How grateful I am that my sins are forgiven, but I didn't realize that still "the flesh wages war against the spirit." I would continue to struggle with sin? "No one can snatch you from the Father's hand." I memorized that promise of eternal security. However, did it also say "in this life, you will have trouble?"

God's Word makes it clear that there is more than meets the eye for a Christian in this life. There are promises and there are responsibilities. There are blessings and there are crosses. There are great rewards, but there is also suffering. We can keep from sinking into murky waters when we anticipate both the pleasures and the challenges. Those who do will get more than they bargained for.

> Things which eye has not seen and ear has not heard, and which have not entered the heart of man, all that God has prepared for those who love him.
>
> 1 CORINTHIANS 2:9, NASB

Lord,
Thank You for both the joys and the trials that are part of my walk with You. Prepare me to accept both with equal peace and grace.

Are You Talking to Me?
~~~~~~

What came to you from God today?
It is worth writing about.

Logging the Miles   Today is _____

One word to describe my day would be _____

The greatest thing about today was _____
_____
_____
_____
_____

The funniest thing that happened today was _____
_____
_____
_____
_____

I was really frustrated by _____
_____
_____
_____
_____

I wish I would have _____
_____
_____
_____
_____

God, I could tell that You were with me today because _____

_____

_____

_____

_____

_____

_____

I'm ready to hear You speak, Lord. What I hear You say through it all is

_____

_____

_____

_____

_____

_____

God, because I heard You, I know that I should _____

_____

_____

_____

_____

_____

A scripture that comes to mind is _____

_____

_____

_____

_____

_____

Day 28
No Sale

Many weeks, the biggest thing on my shopping list is a ten-pound bag of potatoes. I never need ten pounds of potatoes, but they are only fifty cents more than a five-pound bag, so I feel compelled to buy them and put them in my dark pantry, where I will forget about them until they are soft and runny and drawing flies. Then I toss them out, disinfect the pantry, and add potatoes to my shopping list.

It was a rare occasion when I got to add something really big to my list—furniture. A local store was going out of business and had priced their entire stock at 50 percent off. It just so happened that I had a 50-percent-off budget. I also had a desperate need for chairs. With five people in our family, but only one couch and one chair among our possessions, skirmishes frequently ensued. "I call the couch." "Get your feet off my side." "My chair is saved." More often than not, I got a pillow on the floor during movie night. Fifty-percent-off chairs were just what we needed.

At the clearance sale I found the perfect chairs. They were big, roomy, and half price. The extra bonus was that they even matched the room. For three days I visited the store, trying to decide if I should splurge. On the fourth day I took my husband, who didn't gush with enthusiasm, as I had hoped, and I was left doubting. On the fifth day I took a friend, who I was sure would bubble over with excitement and think chenille was the right choice. On the sixth day, the chairs were still there, so I knew they were meant for me. Why else would they still be there?

Before I went to the counter to pay for my new family room chairs, I backed our truck to the front door and left the salesman to load them. Then I made my way to the back of the store, where a clerk entered my purchase on the computer. When he told me the price I opened my checkbook to make my payment, but before I could even write the date I was stopped.

"Sorry, Ma'am. We can't take your check. We're liquidating. Cash or credit cards only."

Cash? Was he trying to be funny? On a good day, I might find enough change for a soda, but furniture? I held out thirty-four cents and a fuzzy mint, but he was not amused, especially since it was closing time on a Friday night.

"Well, we can try this credit card," I told him, "but it's new. I've never used it before."

As he scanned it, the annoying beep of his computer told me I wouldn't be using it that day either. "Sorry, it says your card isn't activated."

Out of options, there was nothing left to do but ask the salesman outside, who had just loaded three heavy chairs into the back of my truck, to unload the heavy chairs and hold them until I could return the next day. It was a pathetic scene.

"I am so sorry.... Yes, I see you just loaded all the furniture.... No, I didn't know I needed cash.... Yes, now I see that big red sign on the door.... I am so, so sorry.... I'll have to come back tomorrow."

"Ma'am," he said decisively, "I'm not unloading all that furniture." He turned to the clerk to confirm that he had recorded my name and phone number on the computer. Then he did something

I did not expect. "Go ahead and take the furniture, since it's already loaded. I'm trusting you to come back in the morning."

Maybe it was my humble groveling. Maybe it was just late. Maybe the guy had a hot date waiting. I didn't ask any questions. I was just glad to have my new chairs, so I left while the offer was still good, thinking, "Tonight I won't have to sit on the floor."

In the middle of arranging and rearranging my new chairs the next morning, the phone rang. It was the salesman. Apparently his boss had a few small concerns about our "take-it-now-pay-later" arrangement. In fact, if I didn't show up with the money by noon, the poor guy was fired.

When I hung up the phone, I realized something I'm sure the salesman had already figured out. His job security was totally dependent on me. What if the banks were closed, or I ran out of gas, or I couldn't get my hair washed in time? It was already 10:30, and even though the store was a mere five minutes away, I worried that I wouldn't make it.

I resisted the temptation to rearrange the furniture just one more time and instead prepared to save my salesman from that fate worse than death—unemployment. In an effort to convince his manager that he had not made a poor decision, I put on a suit, accessorized, and even carried a matching purse. I wanted to appear respectable. Finally I headed to the store.

I have to say that no one has ever greeted me with as much joy as that salesman. The only thing that made him happier was seeing the cash I brought with me. Relief washed over his face as he expressed his gratitude for my timely arrival. He would keep his job after all.

How much God desires us to be like that furniture salesman. He wants us to be utterly dependent on Him, aware that without Him, we are hopeless in every situation.

> We were under great pressure, far beyond our ability to endure, so that we despaired even of life.... But this happened that we might not rely on ourselves but on God, who raises the dead. He has delivered us from such a deadly peril, and he will deliver us.
>
> 2 CORINTHIANS 1:8-10

Utter dependence on God has to be the biggest item on our lists if we are going to experience the joy of God's deliverance in a multitude of ways, big and small.

Lord,
Thank You that You are the supplier of all my needs. Forgive me when I depend on other things, like money, friends, and my own wisdom to give me hope. Right now I give You my concerns and ask You to be my rescuer.

What has God rescued you from today?
Record it on the next page.

Are You Talking to Me?

Logging the Miles   Today is _____

One word to describe my day would be _____

The greatest thing about today was _____

_____

_____

_____

_____

_____

The funniest thing that happened today was _____

_____

_____

_____

_____

_____

I was really frustrated by _____

_____

_____

_____

_____

_____

I wish I would have _____

_____

_____

_____

_____

Are You Talking to Me?

~~~~~~~

God, I could tell that You were with me today because _____

_____

_____

_____

_____

_____

_____

I'm ready to hear You speak, Lord. What I hear You say through it all is

_____

_____

_____

_____

_____

_____

God, because I heard You, I know that I should _____

_____

_____

_____

_____

_____

_____

A scripture that comes to mind is _____

_____

_____

_____

_____

_____

Day 29
Hear Ye

I have a hearing disability. I don't know if it's genetic. I suspect it is, because I see signs of it in my children. Its technical name is Auditory Immune Syndrome, commonly known as selective hearing.

My husband was the first to detect this defect. He noticed it when I consistently reported no recollection of conversations about specific topics. One of these areas is a budget. He says he regularly tells me the importance of staying on one, yet when standing in the middle of the shoe store, I cannot recall such conversations.

I am also immune to topics relating to certain household duties, like cooking and cleaning, and those dealing with personal criticism. I don't actually go as far as sticking my fingers in my ears and humming loudly, but I have been known to turn a deaf ear to such unpleasant topics.

Like many with disabilities, however, my husband quickly points out that I compensate in other areas, like hearing things that he never actually says. "You got your hair cut," somehow reaches me as "I liked it better the other way."

When he says, "Are we eating out again?" I hear, "Are you ever going to cook again?" In these circumstances my keen sense of hearing cuts through the actual words to decipher the intent behind them.

This gift I have of interpreting my husband's tongue may be

directly attributable to my gender. I have not seen research on this, but I believe data would show that all women have this special discernment. Skeptics may say it is just a matter of hearing what we want to hear, but evidence proves otherwise.

As early as my honeymoon, this gift of interpretation began to manifest itself. We chose to spend our honeymoon at Walt Disney World in Florida. This seemed the perfect environment for my very own fairy tale. For months I anticipated what it would be like to spend seven days alone with a man totally committed to my happiness. What better way to start our life than with a week of his undivided attention in our very own wonderland?

You can imagine my disappointment when, after just two days, I heard him say, "I'm bored with you." In the interest of fairness, he swears that what he said was, "Why don't we visit the Space Center?" Yet I knew what he really meant, and it was an ominous sign. One day he puts the space shuttle first; the next day it's ESPN. His devotion was being tested.

What happened next confirmed it. As we were disembarking from our romantic bus ride to the Space Center—with one hundred other tourists—I caught my foot and tumbled down three steps, landing with an ungraceful thud face down on the pavement. My devoted husband, slowed by his interest in the visitor's brochure, was still on the bus.

Finally I looked up to see my knight coming to my rescue. He reached for me, and in a gentle whisper I heard him say, "Honey, get up. Everyone is looking at you." No, really, he said, "Honey, get up. Everyone is looking at you." He insists that he also asked if I was hurt, but I have no recollection of that. Instead I had proof that my earlier interpretation was accurate. I don't hold a grudge though. That was a long time ago, and I bring it up only occasionally now.

Since then my husband has come to accept my gift as a dynamic part of our relationship. He knows that anything he says is subject to interpretation and may or may not be held against him at a future date—that is, if I happen to hear him at all.

Many of us employ that same approach to the Word of God. We pick and choose the truths that make us feel comfortable and stick our fingers in our ears when we hear things we don't like. Even those we do acknowledge, we reserve the right to interpret according to our need at the moment.

Scripture warns of the results of our refusal to accept that "all scripture is God-breathed" and "profitable."

For the time will come when men will not put up with sound doctrine. Instead, to suit their own desires, they will gather around them a great number of teachers to say what their itching ears want to hear. They will turn their ears away from the truth and turn aside to myths.

2 TIMOTHY 4:3-4

But the man who looks intently into the perfect law that gives freedom, and continues to do this, not forgetting what he has heard, but doing it—he will be blessed in what he does.

JAMES 1:25

There is only one cure for a spiritual hearing disability—to believe the Word of God.

Lord,
Forgive me for the times when I have resisted Your Word because it was
not what I wanted to hear. Guide me away from the desire to be enter-

tained by Your Word. Make my heart receptive to Your truth and my ears keen to detect those who teach myths.

What did your ears hear from God today?
Get a pencil and write it down.

Logging the Miles   Today is _____

One word to describe my day would be _____

The greatest thing about today was _____

_____

_____

_____

_____

_____

The funniest thing that happened today was _____

_____

_____

_____

_____

_____

I was really frustrated by _____

_____

_____

_____

_____

_____

Are You Talking to Me?

I wish I would have _____

_____

_____

_____

_____

God, I could tell that You were with me today because _____

_____

_____

_____

_____

I'm ready to hear You speak, Lord. What I hear You say through it all is

_____

_____

_____

_____

_____

God, because I heard You, I know that I should _____

_____

_____

_____

_____

A scripture that comes to mind is _____

_____

_____

_____

_____

Day 30
Alien Abduction

At great risk to my reputation, I am going to recount an amazing tale. I was held captive by alien life forms. It is a shocking story that must be told.

It started when I volunteered to baby-sit a friend's two young children and innocently stumbled into the alien's lair. My friend had just delivered premature twin baby daughters who were still in the hospital. This was the day she and her husband would travel one hundred miles to retrieve the babies and finally bring them home. I would be attending to their four-year-old son and one-year-old daughter until they returned.

When I volunteered, I knew that it would coincide with a deadline for my weekly newspaper column, so I decided to take my laptop and finish my work there. After waving good-bye to the parents, I set out toys for the toddlers and settled into a chair with my computer. Not realizing the danger I was in, I turned my attention to the keyboard. That's when the abduction began.

First the little boy, if that's what he really was, attempted to zombify my brain with his continual hypnotic chants: "This is my Lego. This is my castle. This is my sword. This is my chair. This is my house. This is my shoe," and on and on he went.

As my eyes began to glaze over, my computer screen flashed and then went dark, snapping me back to reality. I spun in my chair and found, not a little girl, but an alien slime monster holding the plug.

With green gunk oozing from its nose, its true form was emerging. I ran to the bathroom for a tissue in hopes that I could keep the creature from further mutating. It worked, but only temporarily. Every five minutes it demanded I wipe it again.

I knew then my life was no longer my own. I was their captive and would be forced to bear the most unspeakable burdens. When the slime monster wasn't pointing to her nose, she was pointing to her rear-disposal-wrapper. She continually leaked from both ends.

Also never ending was that merciless hypnotic chant. "This is my room. This is my computer. This is my bed. This is my ... I'm hungry. We want breakfast."

Flanked by my captors, I was marched to the kitchen, where a familiar scene greeted me. Just as in my own house, there were dishes in the sink, spills on the counter, and sundry messes on the floor. Shaking off my hypnotic state, I looked afresh at the rest of the house and realized that in the rush toward the hospital, the house had been left in a state of kid-induced disarray.

I looked at the hungry aliens and all the messes they had made and then at my laptop. My choice was clear. Break free and incapacitate the aliens with a Barney movie (kryptonite to all preschool creatures), or feed the hungry aliens, straighten up so Mom and twins could come home to an orderly house, and miss my deadline. Their power must have been great, for I chose to remain in their service, but not before calling two servant-hearted friends as reinforcements.

By the time the father arrived to liberate us, we had straightened the house, conquered the laundry, and wiped away the last traces of slimy ooze. Outwardly, at least, we left a normal household with ordinary children, but behind those angelic faces lurked an alien force I had forgotten existed—the needy toddler. Any who dare approach such a creature will invariably be pressed into service.

Such an inescapable calling is not unlike the service to which God Himself calls us. The high calling of our service to one another is sometimes inconvenient, sometimes hard or unpleasant, certainly not glamorous, tiring, and never ending. Responding to it usually involves giving up our own agendas, our resources, or our comfort. Yet we wouldn't be the first to answer that call.

On Jesus' last night of freedom, just hours before the crucifixion, He set aside His role as Master and voluntarily took on the duty of a slave so that He could again teach the disciples the irreplaceable role that service must play in the lives of His followers.

> Now that I, your Lord and Teacher, have washed your feet, you also should wash one another's feet. I have set you an example that you should do as I have done for you.... Now that you know these things, you will be blessed if you do them.
>
> JOHN 13:14-15, 17

If Christ, the one true God in the flesh, is willing to serve in such a way, His followers must also be willing servants. This humble role may feel alien at first, but for those who voluntarily serve even the least, the blessings are out of this world.

Heavenly Father,
I confess that most of the time I would rather be served than serve some-
one else. Give me a servant's heart so that I might reach out to others in
a way that meets their needs. Give me a willing heart to put aside my
own agenda to pursue Yours.

How did God show you His agenda today?
Write about it.

Are You Talking to Me?

Logging the Miles   Today is _____

One word to describe my day would be _____

The greatest thing about today was _____
_____
_____
_____
_____
_____

The funniest thing that happened today was _____
_____
_____
_____
_____
_____

I was really frustrated by _____
_____
_____
_____
_____
_____

I wish I would have _____
_____
_____
_____
_____

Are You Talking to Me?
~~~~~~~

God, I could tell that You were with me today because _____

_____

_____

_____

_____

_____

_____

I'm ready to hear You speak, Lord. What I hear You say through it all is

_____

_____

_____

_____

_____

_____

God, because I heard You, I know that I should _____

_____

_____

_____

_____

_____

_____

A scripture that comes to mind is _____

_____

_____

_____

_____

_____

Day 31
Just Boo-tiful

My whole life has been one long bad hair day. From the moment my mother made me cut my hair in the sixth grade, I have marked the years by awful haircuts.

In my teens it was too bleached; in my twenties, too permed; and in my thirties, too short. I lay the whole fiasco at my mother's feet. Right after I was born, she accidentally dyed her own hair purple. I think she subconsciously blamed me and has unknowingly taken revenge.

When I was in the seventh grade, she assured me that a home perm was just what I needed. I stood in front of the mirror after my mother finished, and what looked back was terrifying.

"It just needs a few days to calm down," she assured me. Prozac would not have calmed that hair down.

By the ninth grade my once wheat-blonde hair was dirty dishwater, and by the tenth grade it was pond-scum brown. That's when mom made another suggestion. She thought putting on a sun-in product would be a good idea. I'll never forget those famous last words.

"Honey, we'll just do it once." That was twenty-five years and two hundred boxes of hair color ago.

Each time I used it, my hair got lighter. By the time I went to college, the glare was blinding. Looking directly at my hair could cause permanent eye damage. It took three years to tone it down to "extra light blonde."

The vicious cycle of destructive hair behavior continued, even after I left home. In my twenties I faced the perm rods again, this time in the hands of professionals. After two good sets, I thought the nightmare was finally over. Then out of nowhere came the "poodle perm." I went in for a wave and came out looking like Fifi.

When my first child was born, I decided it was time to go natural. For three years I let my roots grow out. I came to my senses only after looking at photos of myself with my next baby. Drab hair called for drastic measures. I was back on the bottle within the week (the hair color bottle, that is). I have vowed never to go dishwater brown again.

The darkest day in my hair history came a few summers ago. Though I swore I would never cut my hair short, the day finally came. Surprisingly, my new cut was fashionable and chic, when I left the salon, but by the time I got home, it had fallen like a soufflé. No matter what I tried, it would not re-pouf. My hair was a disaster and I was due at the baseball park to coach a T-ball game.

I sat home, willing it to grow. The only person who understood was my daughter, who cried over my lost hair. My older son told me I looked like a boy. My middle child, watching the others critique my hair, walked all around me, ran his fingers through it, and thought carefully.

"Mom, it will be OK. It looks good under your hat."

Sure, it would be OK. Maybe no one would notice.

They noticed. Even in the middle of the game all I could think about was my horrible, no good, very bad hair. Then one six-year-old boy came running across the field. "Coach, coach!" I waited for him as he ran up breathlessly. "Oh, Coach," he said earnestly, "I just wanted to tell you, I think your hair is boo-tiful, just boo-tiful."

This special little boy was one whom I had poured hugs on all

167

season. He needed encouragement and a little extra attention. We had built a relationship over baseball and laughter and ample words of praise. I knew that while he might have been looking at my hair, it was me to whom he was giving his approval. It was the best compliment I could have received.

I know that I'm not the only one who sometimes feels self-conscious or inadequate. Our insecurities are over more than just our appearances. Our homes, our clothes, our education, our careers, and even our children's accomplishments can be focuses of our insecurities. When we look around, we don't seem to measure up, but that's partly because we are using the wrong measuring stick.

God warned the prophet Samuel not to look at the impressive outward appearance of men when looking for God's choice for king. "The Lord does not look at the things man looks at. Man looks at the outward appearance, but the Lord looks at the heart" (1 Sm 16:7).

His choice would not be one based on social standing, spectacular appearance, or personal achievement. God's measuring stick reaches deep into the soul, measuring things like faith, character, and humility. These are the things that will cause God and others to see us as boo-tiful, even on a bad hair day.

Dear Lord,

Thank You that Your approval does not depend on my outward appearance. I know that it is the beauty of my character that pleases You. Forgive me where I have been more concerned with my outer features and less concerned with the inner ones. With the mirror of Your Word, show me where my heart needs a makeover.

What did God show you today? Turn the page and write all about it.

Logging the Miles   Today is _____

One word to describe my day would be _____

The greatest thing about today was _____

_____

_____

_____

_____

_____

The funniest thing that happened today was _____

_____

_____

_____

_____

_____

I was really frustrated by _____

_____

_____

_____

_____

I wish I would have _____

_____

_____

_____

_____

_____

Are You Talking to Me?

God, I could tell that You were with me today because _____

_____

_____

_____

_____

_____

_____

I'm ready to hear You speak, Lord. What I hear You say through it all is

_____

_____

_____

_____

_____

_____

_____

God, because I heard You, I know that I should _____

_____

_____

_____

_____

_____

A scripture that comes to mind is _____

_____

_____

_____

_____

_____

The Finish Line

Congratulations! For thirty-one days you have invited God on the road with you. By now you probably realize that He has been with you all along. You just couldn't hear Him over all that road noise called "life." Isn't it great to discover that you are not on the journey alone? God is a great companion. He isn't a backseat driver. He doesn't change the radio station. And He never leaves His junk in the car.

What He does do is whisper gently which way you should go. "And your ears shall hear a word behind you, saying, 'This is the way, walk in it,' when you turn to the right or when you turn to the left" (Is 20:31). God knows every twist and turn in the road ahead. There is no one better to have as your guide. It isn't always easy to hear His voice in the whirlwind of your life, but those who listen intently, faithfully, and prayerfully will perceive what He has to say. I hope that is what you have discovered in the past thirty-one days.

Now continue to expect a daily encounter with the God who promises us that if we "draw near to [Him], He will draw near to [us]" (Jas 4:8). Draw near by reading His written word every day. Draw near through prayer and worship. Then draw near by seeking Him on the everyday roads of life, as we have done together for the past month. You can have more than thirty-one days of hearing from God personally. You can have a lifetime!

Kim Wier
is the founder and president of
Engaging Women Ministries
www.Engagingwomen.com

Kim is a newspaper humor columnist,
co-host of Engaging Women Radio Program,
and a Christian speaker and Bible teacher.
Look for her latest book.
*Redeeming the Season: Taking Back Christmas
From Santa and Sears* (September 2002)

**You can schedule Kim to speak to your group by contacting
CLASServices at 1-800-433-6633**

If you would like to write to Kim, she invites you to email to
kim@engagingwomen.com